2009–2010

Unbelievably Good Deals

and **Great Adventures**

That You Absolutely

Can't Get Unless You're

Over 50

2009–2010

Unbelievably Good Deals
and **Great**
Adventures
That You Absolutely
Can't Get Unless You're
Over 50

Joan Rattner Heilman

New York   Chicago   San Francisco   Lisbon   London   Madrid   Mexico City
Milan   New Delhi   San Juan   Seoul   Singapore   Sydney   Toronto

The *McGraw·Hill* Companies

2 3 4 5 6 7 8 9 10 11 12 13 14 15 16 17   WFR/WFR   1 9 8 7 6 5 4 3 2 1 0

ISBN 978-0-07-159884-2
MHID   0-07-159884-7
ISSN 19459408

McGraw-Hill books are available at special quantity discounts to use as premiums and sales promotions or for use in corporate training programs. To contact a representative, please e-mail us at bulksales@mcgraw-hill.com.

This book is printed on acid-free paper.

Contents

1

Good Deals and Great Adventures

This book is a guide to the perks, privileges, and special adventures that are yours simply because you're now at least 50 years old.

On your 50th birthday (or on your 60th, 62nd, or 65th), you qualify for hundreds of special opportunities and money-saving offers that make younger people wish they were older—all for a couple of good reasons. First, as a person in your prime, you deserve them.

Second, as part of the fastest-growing demographic group in the United States, you represent an enormous market of potential consumers. About 4 out of 10 Americans are now over 50, with 10,000 boomers turning 50 every day. About 37 million Americans—about 12 percent of the total population—are now over the age of 65, and it is predicted that by 2030 that number will double to almost 72 million. Life expectancy is higher than ever before, and Americans who survive to age 65 can expect to live an average of 18.7 more years.

1

Those of us over 50 control most of the nation's wealth, including half of the discretionary income (the money that's left over after essentials have been taken care of). Net worth has increased almost 80 percent for older Americans over the past 20 years, according to a government report. Very often, the children have gone, the mortgage has been paid off, the house is fully furnished, the goal of leaving a large inheritance is no longer a major concern, and the freedom years have arrived at last.

As a group, we're markedly different from previous older generations who pinched pennies and saved them all. We know the value of a dollar, but we feel freer to spend because we're more prosperous than our predecessors, a significant number of us having accumulated enough resources to be reasonably secure. In fact, the boomers are the wealthiest group of older people in history. We are far better educated than earlier generations, and we have developed many more interests and activities.

Most important, today's older Americans are fitter and healthier than their parents ever were. We're living longer and feeling better. In fact, a survey has shown that most of us feel at least 15 years younger than our chronological age and rate our health as good or excellent.

The business community targets the mature population because now many of us have the time to spend our money doing all the things we've always put off before. Although many continue to work after age 65, the average age of retirement has dropped. With the recognition of our numbers and financial power, our flexible schedules, and our vast buying power, we are finally being taken very seriously. To get our attention, we are continually presented with real breaks and good deals, all detailed on these pages. We are also invited on trips and adventures tailored to suit our interests, needs, and abilities.

In this book, you will learn how to get what's coming to you—the discounts and privileges that are among the advantages of getting older. Here are some that you absolutely couldn't get if you were younger:

■ Discounts at hotels and motels; at car-rental agencies; and on buses, trains, and boats
■ Bargain rates at colleges and universities
■ Travel adventures all over the world created specifically for older travelers
■ Clubs, trips, and services for mature singles
■ Skiing for half price—or nothing
■ Tennis tournaments, golf vacations, walking trips, bike tours, and senior softball leagues designed for you
■ And much more

Because every community in this country and abroad has its own special perks to offer you, make a practice of *asking* if there are breaks to which you are entitled, from movies to museums, concerts to historic sites, hotels to ski resorts and theme parks, restaurants and buses to riverboats. Don't expect clerks, ticket agents, tour operators, restaurant hosts, or even travel agents to volunteer them to you. First of all, they may not think of it. Second, they may not realize you have reached the appropriate birthday. And third, they may not want to call attention to your age, just in case that's not something you would appreciate. You never know whether you're being offered the best possible deal unless you ask. Many bargains and privileges are available only to people who speak up.

Remember to request your privileges *before* you pay or when you order or make reservations and always carry proof of age, such as a driver's license, an over-50 club membership card, or—better yet—both. Sometimes the advantages come with membership in a senior club, but usually they are available to anyone over a specified age.

To make sure you're getting a legitimate discount when you're using your special privileges, call the hotel, car-rental company, or tour operator and ask what the regular or normal prices are. Find out if there's a special sale or promotion going on. Ask about other discounts—corporate, weekend, government, or auto-club membership breaks, for example. Most important, always ask for *the lowest available rate* at the time you plan to travel and compare that with the discounted senior rate. Then go with the best deal.

With the help of this guidebook, completely revised and updated, you will have a wonderful time and save money too.

2

Travel: Making Your Age Pay Off

People over 50 are the most ardent travelers of all. We travel more often, farther, more extravagantly, and for longer periods of time than anybody else. Since the travel industry discovered these facts, it's been going after our business.

It caters to our age group because we have more discretionary income than people of other ages and more time to spend it. Besides, we are remarkably flexible. Many of us no longer have children in school, so we're free to travel off-peak or whenever we feel the need for a change of scenery. In fact, we much prefer spring and fall to summer. Some of us have retired, and others have such good jobs that we can make our own schedules. We can take advantage of mid-week or weekend slack times when the industry is eager to fill space.

But, best of all, we are energetic, and we're not sitting around in rocking chairs watching the world go by. People over 55 account for one-third of all overnight domestic travel at least 50 miles from home, overseas packaged tours, and hotel/motel nights, as well as 70 percent of bus trips and cruises.

As a group, older Americans aren't content with watching the action. Instead, we like to get right into the middle of it. There's not a place we won't go or an activity we won't try. Though many of us prefer escorted tours, almost half of us choose to travel independently.

Not only that, but we're shrewd—we look for the best deals to the best places. We are experienced comparison shoppers and want the most for our money.

For all of these reasons, we are now offered astonishing numbers of travel-related discounts, reduced rates, special tour packages, and other perks. Many agencies and tour operators have designed all or at least many of their trips to appeal to a mature clientele. Others include seasoned travelers along with everyone else but offer us special privileges.

So many good deals and great adventures are available to you when you are on the move that we'll start off with travel.

But, first, keep in mind:

- Rates, trips, and privileges tend to change at a moment's notice, so check out each of them before you make your plans. Airlines, rental-car agencies, and cruise lines are particularly capricious, and it's hard to tell what they offer from one day to the next. The good deals in this guidebook are those that are available as we go to press.

- Pay for all travel with a major credit card, if possible. If there are problems or disputes, you will have less difficulty resolving them.
- Always ask for your discount or special privilege when you make your reservations or at the time of purchase, order, or check-in. If you wait until you're checking out or settling your bill, it may be too late.
- Remember that your privileges may apply only between certain hours, on certain days of the week, or during specific seasons of the year. Research this before making reservations and always remind the clerk of the discount when you check in or pay your fare. Be flexible when you can and travel during the hours, days, or seasons when you can get the best deals.
- When traveling, it's particularly important to carry identification with proof of age or membership in a senior club. In most cases, a driver's license or passport does the job. In some cases, the organization's membership card, a birth certificate, a resident alien card, or any other official document showing your date of birth will suffice. If you're old enough for a Medicare card or Senior ID card, use that.
- Look before you book. Don't spring for senior discounts without checking out other rates. Often special promotional rates or discounts available to anybody of any age turn out to be better. Ask your travel agent, the ticket seller, or the reservations clerk to figure out the *lowest possible available rate* for you at the time you want to travel.
- Some senior privileges are available whether you make reservations by telephone or online, but frequently they

are not to be found on the websites. If you want them, you or your travel agent must call. On the other hand, they may be available *only* online. The solution is to try it both ways before you make a decision.

■ The age of a "senior" varies from 50 upward. Some special privileges are yours at age 50, usually but not always tied to membership in a senior organization. Others come along later at varying birthdays, so watch for the cutoff points. Also, in most cases, if the person purchasing the ticket or trip is the right age, the rest of the party, a traveling companion, or the people sharing the room are entitled to the same reduced rates.

3

Hotels and Motels: Get Your Over-50 Markdowns

Now that you're over 50, you'll never have to pay full price for a hotel room again. Across the U.S. and Canada and often in the rest of the world, virtually all lodging chains and most individual establishments go out of their way to give you a break on room rates. You don't even have to wait until you're eligible for Social Security to cash in on your maturity because most hotels, inns, and motels offer discounts to you at age 50, usually requiring only proof of age or membership in a senior organization.

What all this means is that you should *never* make a lodging reservation without making sure you are getting a special rate—a senior discount of at least 10 percent or an even better deal.

Because most hotel chains only offer a percentage discount off the regular "rack" rate, which may or may not be lower than other discounted rates, the senior discount isn't always the cheapest route to a hotel room. You may find the best rates through a hotel broker, a half-price program, chain websites, an online discounter, or a hotel chain's own club or by asking the reservations clerk what's available.

The message is, don't get too enthusiastic about your senior privileges until you've investigated all the possibilities and found the *lowest available rate*.

But, first, keep in mind:

- In this rapidly changing world, rates and policies can be altered in a flash, so an update is always advisable.
- Always ask whether there is a senior discount, whether or not one is posted on the website or mentioned in the hotel's literature. You'll find that just about every hotel has one.
- The basic senior discount of 10 percent is about as good as you'll get at budget hotel chains, so take the deal and run. At more expensive hotels, however, it pays to save the paltry 10 or 15 percent senior discount for the times when you can't score a better deal some other way. You can often save more if you pursue all other options.
- Some of the biggest senior discounts are available only with major restrictions such as a 21-day, nonrefundable advance purchase, so make sure you're willing to live with those restrictions before committing yourself.
- Information about discounts is seldom volunteered. In most cases, you must arrange for them when you make your reservations and confirm them when you check in. Do not wait until you're settling your bill because then it

might be too late. Some hotels and motels require that you make advance reservations to get their discounts. "Advance" may mean a considerable period of time such as three weeks, but it may also mean only a week, a day, or even a few hours.

- In some cases, not every hotel or inn in a chain will offer the senior discount. Those that do are called "participating" hotels or motels. Make sure the one you are planning to visit is participating in the senior plan.

- Although many senior discounts are available every day of the year, some are subject to space availability. This means only a limited number of rooms will be reserved for special rates. If these are already booked or are expected to be booked when you want to stay, you won't get your discount. And some hotels have blackout dates during special events or holiday periods when the discount is not available. So always book early, ask for your discount privileges, and try to be flexible on your dates in order to take advantage of them. Your best bets for space are usually weekends in large cities, weekdays at resorts, and nonholiday seasons.

- Many hotels, particularly in big cities and warm climates, cut their prices drastically in the summer. Others that cater mostly to businesspeople during the week try to encourage weekend traffic by offering bargain rates if you stay over a Saturday night. Resorts are often eager to fill their rooms on weekdays.

- Your senior discount is valid in foreign countries at participating locations of many major American hotel chains, such as Choice Hotels International, Holiday Inn, Marriott, Radisson, and Sheraton.

- If you are traveling with children or grandchildren, remember that at many hotels, children under a specified age, usually 16 or 18, may stay in your room for free. And at some big chains, they may eat free, too.
- In addition to the chains, many independent hotels and inns are eager for your business and offer special reduced rates. Always *ask* before making a reservation. Your travel agent should be able to help you with this.
- In most cases, your discount will not be given on top of other special discounts. One is usually all you get.
- Keep in mind that "extras" included at no additional charge are worth money. Some hotel chains include a full hot breakfast rather than the usual unimaginative continental variety. Others provide no-cost high-speed Internet access, free telephone calls, or evening happy hours. Free parking is another option that can save you plenty. Find out about these possibilities by going online or calling the hotels directly.

AMERICAS BEST VALUE INN

A new brand, this group of 800 disparate hotels give a discount of 10 percent to guests 65 or older and also offer savings to members of AARP who qualify at age 50. But because each inn is individually owned, the amount varies from location to location. Call or go online to find out what is offered along your route.

For information: 888-315-2378; www.americasbestvalue inn.com.

AMERIHOST INN

These economy hotels across the country, all with indoor swimming pools, give a discount of up to 10 percent off the

best available room rates to members of AARP and anybody else who is over 60. Continental breakfast is included.
For information: 800-434-5800; www.amerihostinn.com.

BAYMONT INNS & SUITES

Baymont Inns & Suites operates more than 200 affordable properties, most of them located near shopping areas, major highways, restaurants, and entertainment. AARP members get a 10 percent discount on the best available rate at age 50 and so does anyone else who is at least 60. A free breakfast buffet and free high-speed Internet connections are included.
For information: 877-BAYMONT (877-229-6668); www .baymontinns.com.

BEST WESTERN INTERNATIONAL

Members of AARP and CARP, Canada's association for the 50-plus, are eligible for at least 10 percent off the regular rates every day of the week at participating Best Western hotels. The world's largest hotel chain, Best Western has 4,100 properties in 80 countries, each of them independently owned and operated. Most feature free high-speed Internet access, local phone calls, and a continental breakfast.
For information: 800-WESTERN (800-937-8376); www .bestwestern.com.

BUDGET HOST INNS

A network of about 180 mostly family-owned economy inns in the U.S. and Canada, almost all Budget Host Inns offer senior discounts—usually 10 percent off the regular rates—that vary by location. Call the toll-free reservations number and you will be transferred directly to the front desk of the inn you want, where you can ask about the accommodations, facilities, rates, discounts, and directions to the property. *For information:* 800-283-4678; www.budgethost.com.

CAMBRIA SUITES HOTELS

See Choice Hotels International. Brand-new, upscale, and all suites, Cambria Suites Hotels caters to multitasking travelers who need to stay put for a while and want a home away from home. They are found in commercial, airport, and popular leisure locations. A brand of Choice Hotels International, Cambria Suites offers the same three discount options for seniors: 10 percent for 50-plus, 15 percent for AARP members, and 20 to 30 percent for 60-plus. *For information:* 800-4-CHOICE (800-434-6423); www .choicehotels.com.

CANDLEWOOD SUITES

Candlewood Suites, a group of affordable all-suite hotels, will give you discounted rates if you are 62 or more or present proof of membership in a retired person's organization. Catering especially to business travelers, these hotels are pet friendly too. *For information:* 888-CANDLEWOOD (888-226-3539); www.candlewoodsuites.com.

CASTLE RESORTS & HOTELS

Castle's 20 hotels and condominiums in Hawaii, Saipan, Thailand, Guam, and New Zealand offer guests 50 and over a discount of up to 30 percent off the regular rates every day of the year. *For information:* 800-367-5004; www.castleresorts.com.

CHOICE HOTELS INTERNATIONAL

Among the better deals at major hotels are those offered by Choice Hotels, an international group of about 5,200 locations in 40 countries with brand names that include Main-Stay Suites, Sleep Inn, Comfort Suites, Comfort Inn, Quality, Clarion, Econo Lodge, Cambria Suites, Suburban Extended Stay Hotels, and Rodeway Inn. All of them take catering to older travelers very seriously and give you a choice of three excellent options.

For any traveler 60 or older, the Sixty-Plus Rate gives a discount of 20 to 30 percent when you make reservations in advance at any U.S. participating hotel and at the last minute too when space is available. Call the toll-free number and be sure to request the special rate.

If you're not yet 60 or the Sixty-Plus Rate is not available at the hotel you want, ask for the Fifty-Plus Mature Travelers Rate. It takes 10 percent off and is available every day of the week at all Choice hotels with or without advance reservations.

The AARP Rate is a little better, giving members of this estimable organization a discount of 15 percent and a free continental breakfast at age 50 at thousands of participating hotels around the world.

On top of the senior rates, you are also eligible for Choice Hotels' seasonal promotions that give you a chance to save even more.

For information: 800-4-CHOICE (800-424-6423); www.choicehotels.com.

CLARION HOTELS

See Choice Hotels International. These upscale, full-service hotels and resorts—190 of them in 15 countries—have special accommodations for both business travelers and families. All have swimming pools, exercise rooms, business centers, and restaurants. They offer the three Choice Hotels options for seniors: 10 percent off at age 50, 15 percent for AARP members, and 20 to 30 percent for those 60 and over. *For information:* 800-4-CHOICE (800-424-6423); www .choicehotels.com.

COMFORT INN

See Choice Hotels International. You'll find Comforts, about 3,000 of them, around the world, all of them offering reasonable rates and comfortable lodgings. Most provide complimentary continental breakfast, swimming pools, or even exercise facilities. They all offer the same three Choice Hotels options for seniors: 10 percent off for 50-plus, 15 percent for AARP members, and 20 to 30 percent for those 60 or more. *For information:* 800-4-CHOICE (800-424-6423); www .choicehotels.com.

COMFORT SUITES

See Choice Hotels International. These all-suite hotels feature oversized rooms with partially divided sleeping and seating areas, a living/workspace, microwaves, and refrigerators. All have swimming pools or exercise rooms and serve continental breakfast every morning. They all offer the three Choice Hotels options for seniors: 10 percent off for 50-plus, 15 percent for AARP members, and 20 to 30 percent for those 60 or more.

For information: 800-4-CHOICE (800-424-6423); www .choicehotels.com.

COUNTRY HEARTH INN

Most of these economy motels in the South and Midwest take 10 percent off the room rates for visitors over 50.
For information: 800-848-5767; www.countryhearth.com.

COUNTRY INNS & SUITES BY CARLSON

At each of these midprice properties with a warm and cozy country ambience, you are offered a 10 percent discount off the regular rates if you are over the age of 60. All you have to do is ask for it. A complimentary breakfast is included.
For information: 800-456-4000; www.countryinns.com.

COURTYARD BY MARRIOTT

See Marriott Hotels & Resorts. If you're 62 or older, you'll get 15 percent off the regular room rates every day of the year at participating locations of these moderately priced hotels designed for business and leisure travelers. Most hotels feature restaurants, meeting spaces, swimming pools, exercise facilities, and free Internet access. Advance reservations are recommended.
For information: 800-236-2427; www.courtyard.com.

CROWNE PLAZA HOTELS & RESORTS

Every day of the year, Crowne Plaza Hotels around the world will give you discounted rates if you are 62 or older

or present proof of membership in a retired person's organization. Targeted to cater especially to business travelers,
they have business centers, fitness rooms, restaurants,
concierge services, and meeting rooms.
For information: 800-227-6963; www.crowneplaza.com.

DAYS INNS WORLDWIDE

One of the first national brands of economy lodgings in the
country, Days Inns has replaced its September Days Club
with a discount of 10 percent off the best available rates for
members of AARP at age 50 and anybody else who's at least
60.
For information: 800-DAYS-INN (800-329-7466); www
.daysinn.com.

DELTA HOTELS

There is a nice simple way of getting a seniors rate of 10 to
15 percent off the standard rates when you make reservations at any of the 42 Delta Hotels in Canada. Just ask for it,
and have an ID handy to prove you're at least 65 at check-in.
For information: 888-890-3222; www.deltahotels.com.

DOWNTOWNER INNS

See Red Carpet Inn. 800-251-1962; www.bookroomsnow
.com.

DRURY HOTELS

This small group of hotels, mostly in the South and Midwest, has a senior rate for 50-plus travelers, but it varies
according to location and availability. So all we can tell you
is to ask about it when you make your reservations. The

extras include a free hot breakfast, evening beverages and snacks, high-speed Internet access, free local calls, and one hour of free long-distance calls a day.

For information: 800-DRURYINN (800-378-7946); www .druryhotels.com.

ECONO LODGE

See Choice Hotels International. In addition to three varieties of senior discounts, these affordable hotels feature special accommodations for older travelers. Its "senior rooms" feature bright lighting, large-button telephones, easy-to-read alarm clocks, and grab bars in the bathroom. A new feature is the installation of "hot spots" so you can access the Internet. All Econo Lodges offer the three Choice Hotels options for seniors: 10 percent off for 50-plus, 15 percent for AARP members, and 20 to 30 percent for those 60 or more.

For information: 800-4-CHOICE (800-424-6423); www .choicehotels.com.

EXEL INNS OF AMERICA

A small group of budget motels in the Midwest, most Exel Inns offer a 10 percent discount to guests who are 55 and over.

For information: 800-367-3935; www.exelinns.com.

FAIRFIELD INN BY MARRIOTT

See Marriott Hotels International. At this midprice group of hotels, you are eligible for a 15 percent discount on the regular room rates for up to two rooms for an unlimited number of nights when rooms are available, but only if you are 62 or older. A continental breakfast and free Internet access are included.

For information: 800-236-2427; www.fairfieldinn.com.

FOUR POINTS HOTELS BY SHERATON

Four Points Hotels, located in nine countries, are full-service hotels with affordable prices. Like other members of the Starwood group of lodgings, they give a good deal to AARP members—up to 50 percent off the published room rates with a 21-day, nonrefundable advance purchase that includes a Thursday, Friday, or Saturday arrival. Without the advance booking, you can save 15 to 25 percent any day of the week.

For information: 800-368-7764 or 877-778-2277; www .fourpoints.com or www.starwood.com/aarp.

HAMPTON HOTELS

These moderately priced hotels and suites have more than a thousand locations in the U.S., Canada, and Latin America. When you make a reservation, ask for the AARP discount of 10 percent off the lowest available rate. A breakfast buffet and high-speed Internet access are included. Many of the hotels have swimming pools and exercise facilities.

For information: 800-HAMPTON (800-426-7866); www .hampton-inn.com.

HAWTHORN SUITES

This coast-to-coast chain of suites hotels gives a 10 percent discount to travelers 50 and more. Included in the rate are a continental breakfast, social hour, and swimming pool. Besides, most locations welcome pets.

For information: 888-777-7511; www.hawthornsuites.com

HILTON HOTELS

The Senior HHonors travel club, the outstanding deal that Hilton once offered older travelers, has been discontinued, and no new memberships or renewals are accepted. Lifetime members have been morphed into the regular Hilton HHonors program. However, many hotels in the Hilton family offer senior discounts from 5 to 15 percent that vary by hotel and brand name. So check them out when you make a reservation.

For information: 800-HILTONS (800-445-8667) or 800-492-3232; www.hilton.com.

HISTORIC HOTELS OF AMERICA

Historic Hotels of America is a program of the National Trust for Historic Preservation that has identified 203 hotels that have maintained their historic integrity, architecture, and ambience. They must be at least 50 years old, listed in or eligible for the National Register of Historic Places, or recognized locally as having historic significance.

All of these landmark hotels are independently owned and differ on their savings for seniors, but most give visitors over the age of 50 a 10 percent discount and some offer even more.

For information: Call each hotel directly. Or contact National Trust Historic Hotels of America, 1785 Massachusetts Ave. NW, Washington, DC 20036; 800-678-8946 or www .historichotels.org.

HOLIDAY INN AND HOLIDAY INN EXPRESS

At Holiday Inns around the world, you are entitled to discounted rates every day if you are 62 or older or present proof of membership in a retired person's organization.

Amenities at Holiday Inns include swimming pools, restaurants, business services, meeting facilities, and fitness rooms. Holiday Inn Express offers modern accommodations at affordable rates.

For information: 800-HOLIDAY (800-465-4329); www.holiday-inn.com or www.hiexpress.com.

HOWARD JOHNSON INTERNATIONAL

A famous American landmark, Howard Johnson opened its first hotel in 1954 and is now found throughout the U.S. and many other countries. To AARP members who make an advance reservation, its several brands—Howard Johnson Hotels, Howard Johnson Inns, Howard Johnson Express Inns, and Plaza Hotels—give a discount of up to 10 percent off the best available room rates in the U.S. and Canada. To others over the age of 60, they offer a 10 percent discount at participating properties.

For information: 800-I-GO-HOJO (800-446-4656); www.howardjohnson.com.

HYATT HOTELS & RESORTS

In the continental U.S. and Canada, Hyatt Hotels, a collection of upscale lodgings, gives guests who are 62 or older up to 50 percent off the rate of the day, depending on the location and availability. When you make your reservations, ask for the senior rate.

For information: 800-233-1234; www.hyatt.com.

INTERCONTINENTAL HOTELS & RESORTS

InterContinental Hotels, with about 140 properties in 65 countries, offers services and amenities specifically designed for the international business traveler in key destinations around the globe. With upscale restaurants, concierge services, complimentary breakfasts and evening cocktails, meeting rooms, business service centers, fitness centers, and other amenities, participating properties in this group of hotels give a 10 percent discount to guests over 50 on the nondiscounted room rates in the U.S. when space is available.

For information: 800-424-6835; www.intercontinental.com.

KNIGHTS INN

Clean, comfortable, and inexpensive, the Knights Inn properties across the U.S. and Canada take up to 10 percent off the best available room rates for members of AARP and anyone else who is 60 or more.

For information: 800-843-5644; www.knightsinn.com.

LA QUINTA INNS & SUITES

La Quinta Inns are inexpensive and become even more so when you get your 10 to 30 percent senior discount. You'll get it if you are an AARP member or are at least 55 and can prove it. A full continental breakfast, free local calls, and high-speed Internet access are included.

For information: 800-531-5900; www.lq.com.

LOEWS HOTELS

A group of 18 hotels and resorts located in major cities in the U.S. and Canada, Loews has a senior rate for guests 50-plus that takes 5 to 10 percent off the best available rate.

If you're traveling with children, check out the children's programs and the "family concierge" who's there to help you

plan your visit. If you're on the road with a pet, let the hotel know and it will be offered some treats and toys.
For information: 800-23-LOEWS (800-235-6397); www .loewshotels.com.

LUXURY COLLECTION HOTELS

This small group of unique hotels in many countries offers a discount of up to 50 percent off the published room rates to AARP members who make a 21-day, nonrefundable advance purchase with a Thursday, Friday, or Saturday arrival. Without the advance booking, the savings are 15 to 25 percent any day of the week. You may also sign up for complimentary membership in the Starwood Preferred Guest Program at the Preferred Plus Tier, and you can earn points for frequent nights, upgrades, instant rewards, and late checkout.
For information: 800-325-3589 or 877-778-2277; www .luxurycollection.com or www.starwood.com/aarp.

MAINSTAY SUITES

See Choice Hotels International. MainStay Suites offers homey accommodations designed for extended stays with kitchens, dining, and living areas. Most locations have swimming pools, business centers, and exercise rooms. Complimentary breakfast is served weekday mornings. All of these suite hotels give the same three Choice Hotels options for seniors: 10 percent off for 50-plus, 15 percent for AARP members, and 20 to 30 percent for those 60 or more.
For information: 800-4-CHOICE (800-424-6423); www .choicehotels.com.

MARRIOTT HOTELS & RESORTS

Marriott's good deal for seniors is a simple 15 percent savings on standard room rates every day of the week for everybody age 62 or older. It's valid at Marriott properties worldwide, including Marriott Hotels & Resorts, Courtyard by Marriott, Fairfield Inn by Marriott, Renaissance Hotels & Resorts, Residence Inn by Marriott, SpringHill Suites by Marriott, TownePlace Suites by Marriott, and even Marriott Vacation Club International. Subject to availability, the discount is good for up to two rooms for an unlimited number of nights.

For information: 800-228-9290; www.marriott.com.

MASTER HOSTS INNS

See Red Carpet Inn. 800-251-1962; www.bookroomsnow .com.

MERCURE HOTELS

If you're 55 or older, Mercure Hotels in France will give you a double-occupancy room for the price of a single, plus complimentary breakfast for two. The offer is valid all year, subject to availability, and doesn't apply to special seasonal rates. At other locations throughout the world, participating Mercure Hotels offer 55-plus guests a 10 percent discount off the standard room rates but only when the room is booked through a travel agent.

For information: www.mercurehotels.com.

MICROTEL INN & SUITES

At these independently owned, newly constructed economy hotels, all virtually identical and accessible to travelers with disabilities, guests over the age of 50 are eligible for a 10 percent discount off the best available rates at participating locations in the U.S. and elsewhere. Continental breakfast is included as are local and long-distance calls and high-speed Internet access.

For information: 800-771-7171; www.microtelinn.com.

MOTEL 6

Take advantage of a 10 percent discount off the room rates at any of these pet-friendly economy motels in the U.S. and Canada if you're 60 or more. Pets are welcome and stay free. So do children under 18 when they stay in your room. You may save more, however, by going online to check out the periodic special deals.

For information: 800-4-MOTEL6 (800-466-8356); www .motel6.com.

OMNI HOTELS

Omni Hotels offers luxury accommodations with a wide range of amenities at more than 40 hotels and resorts throughout the U.S., Canada, and Mexico. All of its locations offer a Leisure 55 rate—a 10 percent discount off the weekend leisure rates, subject to availability, to guests who are 55 years old and can show proof at check-in.

For information: 800-THE OMNI (800-843-6664); www .omnihotels.com.

PARADORES OF SPAIN

See Spain, Chapter 8.

PARK INN

Economy hotels that cater to both business and leisure travelers, Park Inn locations in the U.S. and Canada will take 10 percent off the standard rates for guests over the age of 60. *For information:* 800-670-7275; www.parkinn.com.

PARK PLAZA HOTELS & RESORTS

Midscale, full-service downtown, suburban, and airport-convenient hotels, Park Plazas offer you a discount of 10 percent off standard room rates at age 60 in the U.S. and Canada and 65 in Europe. You can get it all year, seven days a week, when rooms are available.
For information: 800-814-7000; www.parkplaza.com.

PASSPORT INNS

See Red Carpet Inn. 800-251-1962; www.bookroomsnow.com.

POUSADAS OF PORTUGAL

See Portugal, Chapter 8.

QUALITY INNS, HOTELS & SUITES

See Choice Hotels International. This group of about 900 full-service lodgings all over the world offers a range of amenities, such as a hot buffet breakfast, in addition to the usual Choice Hotels discounts for seniors: 10 percent off for 50-plus, 15 percent for AARP members, and 20 to 30 percent for those 60 or more.
For information: 800-4-CHOICE (800-424-6423); www.choicehotels.com.

RADISSON HOTELS & RESORTS

At Radisson Hotels, you can always get a 10 percent senior discount at age 60 in the U.S., Canada, and Latin America, all year, every day of the week, if rooms are available. In Europe the qualifying age is 65. No club to join, just be ready to show proof of age.

For information: 800-333-3333; www.radisson.com.

RAMADA WORLDWIDE

Spend the night at a Ramada Limited, a Ramada Inn, or an upscale, full-service Ramada Plaza Hotel, and you're entitled to a 10 percent discount off the regular rates if you belong to AARP or are over 60. Breakfast is included.

For information: 800-2-RAMADA (800-272-6232); www .ramada.com.

RED CARPET INN

Almost all of the independently owned, affordable, limited-service inns in the Hospitality International group have a discount for guests over the age of 50, usually 10 percent off the room rates, subject to availability. Most include a complimentary continental breakfast and parking right in front of your door. Located off major highways and suburban byways throughout the U.S. and Canada, they include Red Carpet Inn, Passport Inn, Downtowner Inns, Master Hosts Inns, and Scottish Inns.

For information: 800-251-1962; www.bookroomsnow.com.

RED LION HOTELS & INNS

Mostly located on the West Coast, Red Lion Hotels and Red Lion Inns give a 10 percent discount off the best available

rate to anybody who is at least 50. They range from upper- and midscale, full-service hotels to small inns and all-suites properties, all of which invite you to bring your pet.
For information: 800-RED-LION (800-733-5466); www .redlion.com.

RED ROOF INNS

At age 60, you'll get a 10 percent discount off the regular rates at more than 350 of these pet-friendly budget motels across the country. You can often save even more money by checking out the "Red Hot Deals" on the website for current specials.
For information: 800-RED-ROOF (800-733-7663); www .redroof.com.

RENAISSANCE HOTELS & RESORTS

See Marriott Hotels & Resorts. After your 62nd birthday, you qualify for a 15 percent discount on the regular room rates every day of the week, subject to availability. It's valid for up to two rooms for an unlimited number of nights at any of these upscale lodgings, part of the Marriott Hotel group, in the U.S. and Canada. Just ask for it when you make reservations.
For information: 888-236-2427; www.renaissancehotels .com.

RESIDENCE INN BY MARRIOTT

See Marriott Hotels & Resorts. These long-stay all-suite accommodations, complete with kitchens and separate living areas are made for staying many nights. They offer guests age 62 or over a 15 percent discount on regular rates every day of the year at participating locations. Complimentary continental hot breakfast, evening social hours, and free Internet access are included.

For information: 888-236-2427; www.residenceinn.com.

RESORTQUEST HAWAII

ResortQuest Hawaii operates a diverse collection of 26 hotels and all-suite condominiums in the Hawaiian Islands. Formerly Aston Hotels & Resorts, participating locations in the lodging group give guests 50 years and older up to 30 percent off the standard rates. As with most senior plans, only one person in the traveling party must be 50 to qualify for the Hawaii 5-0 Program. Children stay and eat free.

For information: 877-997-6667; www.resortquesthawaii .com.

RODEWAY INNS

See Choice Hotels International. Rodeway Inns feature Senior Rooms with bright lighting; grab bars in the bathroom; and large buttons on telephones, remote controls, and alarm clocks. Complimentary continental breakfast is part of the package as well as the usual Choice Hotels discounts for seniors: 10 percent off for 50-plus, 15 percent for AARP members, and 20 to 30 percent for those 60 or more.

For information: 800-4-CHOICE (800-424-6423); www .choicehotels.com.

SANDMAN HOTELS

All located in western Canada, this small group of inns gives year-round preferred room rates for guests age 55 or over, when space is available. Ask for the senior rate, or better yet, sign up for the free 55 Plus Senior Program that guarantees you'll get a significant reduction whenever you book a room.

For information: 800-726-3626; www.sandmanhotels.com.

SCOTTISH INN

See Red Carpet Inn. 800-251-1962; www.bookroomsnow .com.

SETTLE INNS AND SUITES

A small family of economy hotels in the Midwest, Settle Inns gives seniors 10 percent off the regular rates and a complimentary breakfast.

For information: 800-677-3060; www.settleinn.com.

SHERATON HOTELS & RESORTS

All of the upscale Sheratons in 70 countries around the world offer you an outstanding break at age 50 if you are a member of AARP. It's a discount of up to 50 percent off the published room rates when you book a stay that includes a Thursday, Friday, or Saturday arrival and make a nonrefundable reservation at least 21 days in advance. If you can't plan that far ahead, you can get the everyday senior discount of 15 to 25 percent off.

For information: 800-325-3535 or 877-778-2277; www .sheraton.com or www.starwood.com/aarp.

SHILO INNS

These affordable hotels, most of them located along major highways in the western states, will give you a 10 percent discount if you have an AARP card or are over the age of 62.

The majority serve a continental breakfast, and all of the inns are dog-friendly.
For information: 800-222-2244; www.shiloinns.com.

SLEEP INN

See Choice Hotels International. At these hotels scattered throughout the world, amenities include a complimentary continental breakfast and the three Choice Hotels options for seniors: 10 percent off for 50-plus, 15 percent for AARP members, and 20 to 30 percent for those 60 or more.
For information: 800-4-CHOICE (800-424-6423); www .choicehotels.com.

SONESTA HOTELS & RESORTS

All of Sonesta's collection of six upscale hotels in Boston, Miami, New Orleans, and Orlando give 10 to 15 percent off the regular rates to AARP cardholders.
For information: 800-SONESTA (800-766-3782); www .sonesta.com.

SPRINGHILL SUITES BY MARRIOTT

See Marriott Hotels & Resorts. Make a reservation at one of these all-suite, moderately priced hotels and, at age 62, you'll get a 15 percent discount on the regular rate for up to two rooms for an unlimited number of nights, when space is available. Included in the package are a complimentary continental breakfast, a business center, an indoor pool, and free local phone calls.
For information: 888-236-2429; www.springhillsuites.com.

ST. REGIS HOTELS

A small group of five-star luxury lodgings, these elegant hotels offer a discount of up to 50 percent to members of AARP who make a 21-day, nonrefundable advance purchase with a Thursday, Friday, or Saturday arrival. If you can't plan so far ahead, you are entitled to a 15 to 25 percent discount any day of the week.

For information: 877-787-3447 or 877-778-2277; www .stregis.com or www.starwood.com/aarp.

STAYBRIDGE SUITES

Designed for extended stays, Staybridge Suites are residential-style hotels with amenities that include fully equipped kitchens, complimentary breakfast, and 24-hour business services with complimentary PC workstations and free Internet access. Anyone 62 or older, or who provides proof of membership in a senior organization, gets a discounted rate any day of the year, subject to availability.

For information: 800-238-8000; www.staybridge.com.

SUBURBAN EXTENDED STAY HOTEL

See Choice Hotels International. These affordable lodgings designed for extended stays have fully equipped kitchens, weekly housekeeping service, Internet access, on-site washers and dryers, and free continental breakfast. Travelers 50-plus get a 10 percent discount, AARP members get 15 percent off, and those over 60 are entitled to 20 to 30 percent off the rates.

For information: 800-4-CHOICE (800-424-6423); www .choicehotels.com.

SUPER 8 MOTELS

One of the world's largest economy lodging chains, with about 1,200 participating motels throughout the U.S. and Canada, Super 8 gives a discount of 10 percent off its regular rates to members of AARP and other guests over 60. You must make advance reservations.

For information: 800-800-8000; www.super8.com.

TOWNEPLACE SUITES BY MARRIOTT

See Marriott Hotels & Resorts. Moderately priced all-suite hotels, TownePlace Suites caters to guests who plan extended stays. It offers townhouse exteriors, full kitchens, outdoor pools, 24-hour exercise rooms, business centers, and a welcome to your pet. And guests 62 and older get a 15 percent discount at participating locations for up to two rooms for an unlimited number of nights when space is available.

For information: 888-236-2427; www.townehousesuites .com.

TRAVELODGE HOTELS

All Travelodge brands—Travelodge, Thriftlodge, Travelodge Inns, Travelodge Hotels, and Travelodge Suites, almost 600 locations ranging from budget to full-service accommodations—have a nice, straightforward plan for older travelers in the U.S. and Canada. Members of AARP or CARP receive 10 percent off at participating locations anytime, any night, with advance reservations. Or there's 10 percent off when space is available for anyone over 60 who arrives with or without reservations. At these hotels, you will get the best publicly available rate for the same accommodations and date or you get your first night free.

For information: 800-578-7878; www.travelodge.com.

W HOTELS

A group of intimate, upscale, downtown hotels with high-tech amenities for business travelers, fitness rooms, spa services, and stylish restaurants, W Hotels has 19 locations in major cities, including five in New York. As part of the Starwood family of hotels, it gives members of AARP a discount of up to 50 percent off the published room rates with a 21-day, nonrefundable advance booking and a Thursday, Friday, or Saturday arrival. Without the advance paid reservation, members save up to 25 percent any day of the week.

For information: 877-778-2277; www.whotels.com or www.starwood.com

WESTIN HOTELS

Westin Hotels, a Starwood brand, offers substantial discounts of up to 50 percent off to members of AARP who book 21 days or more in advance and arrive on a Thursday, Friday, or Saturday. Otherwise there's a discount of 15 to 25 percent every day of the week, when rooms are available.

For information: 800-WESTIN-1 (800-937-8461) or 877-778-2277; www.westin.com or www.starwood.com.

WINGATE BY WYNDHAM

Wingate Inns are new, moderately priced hotels with free high-speed Internet access in every room and 24-hour self-service business centers. Other amenities include complimentary breakfast and exercise facilities. Wingate gives a 5 to 15 percent discount to members of AARP and anybody who's 60 or more.

For information: 877-999-3223; www.wingateinns.com.

WOODFIN SUITE HOTELS

This small group of 17 upscale, all-suites hotels, including Chase Suite Hotels, was designed especially for business travelers and features 24-hour business centers, fitness centers, swimming pools, and whirlpool spas. Each hotel also gives you a discount up to 30 percent off the standard rates if you are at least 62 or can show an AARP card. Included at most locations are a complimentary daily full breakfast and cocktail hour Monday through Thursday evenings. Besides, most locations will also welcome your pet.

For information: 800-966-3346; www.woodfinsuitehotels .com.

WORLDHOTELS

A collection of about 500 hotels and resorts in 80 countries, ranging from deluxe and first-class to affordable, WORLD-HOTELS has a special 60+ Senior Rate. Ask for it when you make reservations at any of these independently owned, one-of-a-kind establishments. It gives you up to 25 percent off the standard rates, plus amenities, such as complimentary breakfast and a room upgrade, that vary by participating hotel.

For information: 800-223-5652; www.worldhotels.com.

WYNDHAM HOTELS & RESORTS

Wyndham's offer to mature guests is generous and simple. At most of these upscale, full-service properties—including Wyndham Luxury Resorts—throughout the U.S., Canada, Mexico, and the Caribbean, AARP members get 35 to 40 percent off the standard room rates at participating locations every day of the year.

For information: 877-999-3223; www.wyndham.com.

4

Alternative Lodgings for Thrifty Wanderers

If you're willing to be innovative, imaginative, and occasionally fairly spartan, you can travel for a song or thereabouts. Here are some novel lodging options that can save you money and perhaps offer adventures in the bargain. Not all of them are designed exclusively for people over 50, but each reports that the major portion of its clientele consists of free spirits of a certain age who like to travel, appreciate good value for their money, and enjoy getting to know new people from other places.

For more ways to cut travel costs and get smart at the same time, check out the residential/educational programs in Chapter 13.

AFFORDABLE TRAVEL CLUB
Join this bed-and-breakfast club limited to people over 40 and you'll pay a pittance for accommodations, meet

interesting people, and see new places. As a member, you will act as host for fellow members, putting them up in your spare bedroom perhaps a couple of times a year and providing breakfast and a little of your time to acquaint your guests with the area. Visitors pay $15 for a single or $20 for a double per room per night for their stay, and $10 for each additional person. When you travel, you stay in other members' homes.

There are currently about 1,800 member households in this club in 47 states and 50 countries offering accommodations ranging from simple bedrooms to suites and condos. For a membership fee of $70 a year, U.S. hosts receive a newsletter twice a year ($65 online) and an annual printed directory plus two updates a year from which you choose your own hosts and where others may choose you, with mutual agreement, of course. Annual dues for foreign hosts are only $20.

If you have a pet, you may want to take advantage of the club's house-sitting and pet-sitting service—members move into your house and care for your house and/or pets while you're on vacation, meanwhile enjoying a visit to your neighborhood in exchange and no money changes hands.
For information: Affordable Travel Club, 6556 Snug Harbor Ln., Gig Harbor, WA 98335; 253-858-2172; www.affordable travelclub.net.

DEL WEBB'S SUN CITIES

The largest builder of active adult communities, Del Webb offers its Vacation Getaways program at a few of its properties, with the details differing with place and season. These are low-cost, short vacation stays so you can sample the lifestyle to see whether you'd like to move in. Reservations are required. In some communities, you'll stay in your own guest house on site for up to three days. In others, you'll stay at a discounted rate at a nearby hotel, spend time with the residents, try out the facilities and the restaurants, perhaps play a round of golf, explore the clubhouses, and tour the model homes.

The requirements are that one partner in a visiting couple must be at least 55 years old, no one in the group may be younger than 19, guests may stay no more than twice at the same location and must agree to meet with a sales representative during the stay.

For information: Del Webb's Sun Cities, 800-433-5932; www.delwebb.com.

EVERGREEN BED AND BREAKFAST CLUB

This bed-and-breakfast club, exclusively for people over the age of 50, has about 4,000 members and 2,000 host locations in the U.S. and Canada plus a handful of other countries. Whether a host home is elegant or simple, members pay only $10 for a single or $15 double for each overnight stay and bountiful breakfast. In return, they welcome members of the club into their own homes as often as they wish.

Twice a year Evergreen publishes directories of host families that include relevant information about the hosts and the neighborhood. Members use the contact information to arrange their own stays directly with their hosts. A quarterly newsletter provides the latest information. Annual club dues are $60 for a single and $75 for two. You pay only half your first year.

Joining a hospitality club like this one gives you a chance to make new friends and perhaps travel together, as many members do.

For information: Evergreen Bed and Breakfast Club, PO Box 194, Franklin Grove, IL 61031; 800-962-2392 or 815-456-3111; www.evergreenclub.com.

HOSTELLING INTERNATIONAL–CANADA

A network of hostels throughout the Canadian provinces, HI–Canada offers members of all ages an inexpensive night's sleep in a wide variety of places ranging from modern facilities to historic homes, and refurbished jails to log cabins in the Rockies. Located in all major gateway cities and also in remote locations, your accommodations—private or shared—cost very little. Membership for Canadian residents over 18 costs $35 (Canadian) per year and allows you to use any HI facility worldwide at a special discount. No senior discount here, but at these rates, who needs it?

For information: Hostelling International–Canada, 205 Catherine St., Ste. 400, Ottawa, ON K2P 1C3; 800-663-5777 (Canada only) or 613-237-7884; www.hihostels.ca.

HOSTELLING INTERNATIONAL–USA

This international organization, once known as American Youth Hostels, offers low-cost lodging all over the globe to people of all ages. Membership for U.S. adults costs $28 a year, but if you are 55 or more, you pay only $18. You get a membership card, a free guide to hostels in the U.S., and a free map. For an added fee, you may order a guidebook listing more than 4,000 hostels in more than 60 countries, including about 80 in the U.S., in accommodations that range from a lighthouse in California to a modern hotel in mid-Manhattan.

Although most people think of hostels as drab dormitories for backpackers, many these days are in hotels and inns that cater to more upscale travelers and offer private rooms with ensuite bathrooms that can be reserved in advance. Many older, more sophisticated travelers are looking for affordable lodgings but want their comfort and privacy too. Some hostels are located in castles, former dude ranches, convents, base camps, and other exotic places.

There are also Gateway City Hostels in many major cities, including New York; Los Angeles; San Francisco; Miami Beach; Washington, D.C.; Chicago; Seattle; and San Diego. All are centrally located, offer private rooms, and have the services of a program director.

For information: Hostelling International–USA, 8401 Colesville Rd., Silver Spring, MD 20910; 301-495-1240; www .hiusa.org.

ROBSON COMMUNITIES

The Preferred Guest Program at Robson's six villages for active adults in Arizona and Texas offers prospective homeowners a low-cost three-night, weekday stay for two in your own house, with a complimentary dinner, a free round of golf, use of all the recreational amenities, and your own golf cart and bicycles so you can explore on your own. You may use the clubhouse, swimming pools, tennis courts, spas, and golf courses. Of course, visitors will also spend a few hours talking with a salesperson.

The requirements for a visit are that one person in your party must be at least 40 and no one may be under 19.

For information: Robson Communities, 9532 E. Riggs Rd., Sun Lakes, AZ 85248; 800-732-9949; www.robson.com.

US SERVAS

US Servas is the American chapter of Servas International, the oldest and largest free hospitality exchange program in the world. It is a network of thousands of hosts and travelers of all ages in 125 countries who may visit one another for one- or two-night home stays with no charge as a way to promote friendship and understanding among people of diverse cultures. The visits are mutually arranged by the travelers and hosts, using lists of members in the U.S. or abroad.

To be accepted into the program, potential members must be interviewed by local volunteers and provide two letters of reference. Once approved, they are considered to be "ambassadors of peace" and are expected to share their lives, interests, and concerns about social issues. Membership fees are $50 a year for domestic travelers, $85 for international travelers.

For information: US Servas, 1125 16th St., Arcata, CA 95521; 707-825-1714; www.usservas.org.

WCI COMMUNITIES

The Preferred Guest Getaways offered at more than 50 WCI adult villages in six eastern states are designed to show potential homebuyers what they're getting. Sign up for a getaway for a couple of days and you get lodging at a nearby luxury hotel, access to all of the facilities and restaurants, complimentary rounds of golf, and an escorted tour of the community. The cost, which varies widely depending on the location and the season, is always a bargain.

For information: 800-WCI-4005; www.wcicommunities .com.

WELCOME TRAVELLER

A bed-and-breakfast network, Welcome Traveller is an Internet-based club whose members offer hospitality to others who are traveling in their part of the world and accept hospitality when they're on the road. A way to meet people, show them around the neighborhood, share mutual interests, and save money, the club now has about 1,200 members, mainly in the U.S. and Canada, who may act as hosts and/or guests. Guests staying in other members' homes are asked to pay their hosts an honorarium to cover costs. The member database, constantly updated, is sorted into groups according to the members' special interests, vocations, and hobbies, so that hosts and guests will have something in common when they visit. Everyone is free to be included in as many categories as he or she wishes and/or to belong to a nonexclusive general branch that's open to all regardless of particular interests. Current categories include educators, model railroaders, crafters and quilters, runners, women, and 50-plus. Membership is free.

For information: www.welcometraveller.org.

WOMEN WELCOME WOMEN WORLDWIDE (WWWWW)

If you're a traveling woman who'd like to make friends with women all over the world, join Women Welcome Women

Worldwide (WWWWW), a hospitality exchange club whose 3,000-or-so members of all ages in 83 countries welcome one another as guests in their homes. Using the club's directory, hostesses and guests negotiate their own terms for visits, usually for one or two days but sometimes longer. Men may go along too—they just can't join the club. Headquartered in London and financed by member donations (a yearly donation of at least 37 pounds, or about $70 US, is requested), WWWWW also organizes "gatherings" and tours throughout the year. Three newsletters keep you up to date. If you're not a traveler but want to meet women from other places, you may opt to stay home and invite others to come to visit you.

For information: WWWWW, 88 Easton St., High Wycombe, Buckinghamshire HP11, 1LT, UK; www.women welcomewomen.org.uk.

5

Airfares: No Longer So Friendly

nly a few years ago, the skies were very friendly to seniors. All of the major airlines were eager for our patronage and courted us assiduously, first by offering a 10 percent discount off almost all fares to anyone age 62 or over. And then by selling us those much-loved packets of senior coupons for a low flat fee, often saving us considerable amounts of money, especially on long hauls.

Today, however, those special privileges have almost completely vanished. Just one U.S. carrier and a few foreign airlines continue to give seniors a break and sometimes only on their highest fares.

Look before you book:

■ For the best fares and the most available seats, book your travel as early as possible. Discounted seats are limited and may not be reserved at all on some flights. Remember that airfares and airline policies can change overnight, and often do.

■ Some special fares must be booked online, some require you to call, and others aren't posted at all, so you must ask for them. Often the lowest fares are available only online, so cover your bets by checking everything before you buy.

■ Keep in mind that the restrictions you must fly by may not be worth the savings you get with a cheap ticket. Always examine the fees and conditions and decide whether you can live with them. There may be departures only on certain days or at certain hours, restrictions on the season of the year, or stiff penalties for flight changes. It's not always easy to sort out the offers.

■ Be flexible. To get seats and the best fares, plan to fly at off-peak times when the rest of the population isn't rushing off to faraway places. For example, noontime or late-night flights can be much cheaper than early morning or dinnertime flights. Consider leaving on a different day—fares are often lower midweek or on Saturday. Avoid Monday mornings and Friday afternoons. And fly off-season, when children aren't on vacation and there are no major holidays, to get better prices.

■ For cheaper airfares, check out the many low-cost airlines. They may have limited routes and may not fly out of a city or airport that's convenient for you, but they usually offer other important advantages besides cheap tickets. For example, on some of these niche airlines, you may fly only one way and pay just half the round-trip fare, book your trips at the very last minute without penalty, and have no worries about Saturday-night or minimum stays.

■ Some European airlines give senior discounts on fares for domestic flights within their borders or to other cities in Europe. To get the breaks, it is usually necessary to book these flights at the same time and in conjunction with your international ticket.

U.S. AIRLINES

CONTINENTAL AIRLINES

Continental's Presidents Club, with its collection of 27 private airport lounges, is the only VIP club that continues to sell lifetime memberships to those over 62 at about half the regular fee. Check it out if you like to spend your airport waiting time in comfort, complete with snacks and free drinks, luggage storage areas, guest privileges, comfortable seating, and reading material. Members may use their privileges at more than 40 affiliated clubs too.

For information: Continental Presidents Club, 800-322-2640; www.continental.com.

SOUTHWEST AIRLINES

The sole surviving good deal for senior flyers in this country comes from Southwest Airlines, a no-frills, low-cost carrier that flies coast to coast to about 64 cities. If you're 65, you can fly wherever Southwest goes and get 20 to 67 percent off the regular adult fare. You may travel on almost all routes any day of the week, although the number of seats at these special rates is limited, and seats may not be available when you want them, especially on weekends and holidays.

So book as early as possible, and be flexible on your dates and departure times.

If you manage to book a senior ticket, you also get some additional privileges that make your travels less complicated. For example, you may purchase a one-way ticket, eliminating concern about minimum or maximum stays. You can order tickets online and by telephone. There is no advance-purchase requirement, so you can buy them at the last minute. There's no Saturday-night-stay requirement, and, best of all, no charge for changing flights or cancelling at any time right up to departure. Who could ask for anything more?

Remember, however, that the cheapest regular tickets and periodic sale fares for any age can often be less expensive than the senior fares although they have many more restrictions.

Reminder: you must present proof of your age when you check in at the ticket counter for your first flight with Southwest. Ask to become age-verified so that on future travel you can check in 24 hours before your flight.

For information: 800-435-9792; www.southwest.com.

UNITED AIRLINES

United's Silver Wings Plus, the very last senior program offered by a major U.S. airline, has been discontinued, and, except for lifetime members, all membership benefits have been terminated. If you are a lifetime member of the program, however, you will continue to have access to special zone fares and relaxed restrictions. Call United Airlines directly for your reservations and use your current Silver Wings Plus member number.

For information: 800-241-6522; www.united.com.

GOOD DEALS ON FOREIGN AIRLINES

A few foreign airlines still offer a 10 percent discount to passengers at age 60 or 62 on transatlantic flights originating in the U.S., and sometimes a younger companion may get the same deal. Some will also give you a break on domestic flights within their nation's borders. Remember that seasonal promotional rates that are available to travelers of all ages may be lower than the senior fare that is usually based on the highest fares, so be sure to do your homework before committing yourself.

AEROMEXICO

Mexico's largest airline, Aeromexico, flies between 15 destinations in the U.S. and 43 cities in Mexico. It gives 62-plus passengers a 10 percent discount off some fares on its across-the-border flights.

For information: 800-237-6639; www.aeromexico.com.

AUSTRIAN AIRLINES

The Austrian Airlines Group serves 130 cities in 66 countries on five continents. On its frequent two-class, nonstop service across the Atlantic to Vienna and beyond from its gateway cities (New York, Toronto, and Washington, D.C.), it offers a 10 percent discount to passengers 62 and over—and a travel companion of any age—on many regular fares.

For information: 800-843-0002 in the U.S.; 888-817-4444 in Canada; www.austrianair.com.

CATHAY PACIFIC AIRWAYS

The 55 Plus Worry Free Fares from Cathay are not always less expensive than the lowest promotional fares for all ages,

but they have fewer restrictions. Offered to Asia-bound travelers who have turned 55 and have U.S. passports, they are specially priced fares for flights from Los Angeles, New York, or San Francisco to Hong Kong plus one of the following cities: Beijing, Cebu, Delhi, Hanoi, Ho Chi Min City, Jakarta, Manila, Mumbai, Shanghai, Singapore, Taipei. Or from New York to Vancouver on Canada's west coast. You may change your flight free of charge and get a full refund for cancellations anytime prior to departure. Tickets must be purchased online, and reservations made four days in advance.
For information: 800-233-2742; www.cathayusa.com.

EL AL ISRAEL AIRLINES

El Al, Israel's national airline, flies four times more weekly nonstop flights to Israel from the U.S. than any other airline. It offers passengers over 60 and their spouses over 55 special senior fares that are 10 percent, and occasionally even 15 percent, off nonpromotional coach fares between the two countries.
For information: 800-223-6700; www.elal.com.

FINNAIR

Finnair no longer gives older passengers a break on transatlantic flights, but it does give them a maximum stay of 12 months. On flights within Finland or between Finland and other destinations in Europe, however, seniors are eligible for substantial discounts starting at age 65.
For information: 800-950-5000; www.finnair.com.

LUFTHANSA GERMAN AIRLINES

You can still book a transatlantic flight and connecting flights on Lufthansa 10 percent cheaper than the compara-

ble adult rate but only on unrestricted expensive published fares. So it works best to use it only as a fallback when cheaper fares sell out and it's imperative that you fly *now*.
For information: 800-645-3880; www.lufthansa-usa.com.

MEXICANA AIRLINES

All you need is membership in AARP to save 10 to 12 percent on flights originating in the U.S. to many destinations in Mexico. In addition, if you are at least 60, Mexicana offers you a 10 percent discount off the cost of your tickets.
For information: 888-291-1757; www.mexicana.com.

SCANDINAVIAN AIRLINES SYSTEM (SAS)

SAS continues to offer a senior discount of 10 percent for transatlantic passengers 62-plus on flights originating in the U.S. but only on the most expensive full fares. So unless you're traveling at the last minute and must book one of these fares, forget it. The best discounted fares can usually be found on the website.
For information: 800-221-2350; www.flysas.com.

SWISS INTERNATIONAL AIR LINES

Switzerland's airline offers a 10 percent discount to passengers 62 or older and a travel companion each but only on the highest unrestricted fares on flights from the U.S. to its many European destinations. Both passengers must travel together for the entire journey. You can almost certainly find a lower rate unless you require extreme flexibility or are flying at the last minute.
For information: 877-FLY-SWISS (877-359-7947); www
.swiss.com.

6

Beating the Costs of Car Rentals

Never rent a car without getting a discount or a special promotional rate. Almost all car-rental agencies in the U.S. and Canada give breaks to all manner of customers, including those who belong to over-50 organizations or have reached a certain birthday. The discount that's coming to you as a senior member of society can save you some money, although short-term sales will almost always save you more. Refer to the membership material sent by the group to which you belong for information about your discount privileges.

It's almost impossible to sort out the confusing choices of rates, discounts, and add-on fees from the rental companies. To save money, you must shop around, compare costs, and make many decisions that can raise or lower your bill. In general, the best rates are to be found online. When applicable, add the senior discount for renters over 50. It may not amount to much, but it will help a little.

But, first, keep in mind:

- Car-rental agents may not always volunteer information about senior discounts or special sales, so always ask about them when you reserve your car.
- Don't settle for a senior discount or senior rate too hastily without investigating the possibility of an even better deal. Shop around yourself or ask your travel agent to find the *lowest available rate or package* at the time you are going to travel. Ask for the total price that includes all extra charges such as airport fees, taxes, and drop-off fees. Senior discounts are usually given on the full published rental rate. So special promotional rates—in other words, sales—or even weekend rates are almost always better, sometimes much better. On the other hand, if you can get the senior discount *on top of the lowest posted rate*, regular or promotional, that's the deal you want.
- Compare rates from a few agencies because costs can vary greatly.
- Age matters when you want to rent a car. In the U.S., there is usually no maximum age for renters, but that's not the case in many other countries where drivers over a certain age are denied rental vehicles even by American car rental companies. Upper age limits are usually set by the nation's government or the rental agencies and vary according to location. In Ireland, for example, it's doubtful you can find a car to drive if you're 65 or over. One major rental agency won't rent cars to older drivers in 10 countries and another

imposes age limits in 13 foreign countries. Countries where upper age limits may be an issue include Ireland, Italy, Israel, Britain, Greece, Cyprus, Malta, Egypt, and Morocco, but you can never be certain anywhere. Besides, policies concerning age may vary by rental company. One way around this problem, if your stay is going to be more than 17 days, is to lease a car. It can end up cheaper than renting and age is not an issue.

- Book your car as far in advance as you can, especially if you are traveling during a holiday season. Generally, the later you book the more expensive it will be and the less likely you are to get the car you want. If, closer to departure, you find a better rate that suits your needs, you can rebook your reservation.
- Remember that weekly and weekend rates are less expensive than daily rates.
- Most of the major car-rental companies offer weekly specials linked to those of the major domestic airlines. Remember to check them out if you are flying to the city where you will pick up your car.
- Be especially cautious if you are planning a one-way rental because rates can be outrageously high for picking up a car in one city and returning it in another.
- If you have access to the Internet, check the rental agencies' websites for special deals and last-minute offers.
- Before driving away in your rented car, inspect it for dents, scratches, or other damage. If you find any, ask the agent to sign a statement on the condition of the car and attach it to your rental agreement. That way, you won't be in danger of being charged for the damage on your return.

- Ask if there is an additional-driver fee, and don't sign up for it if you don't need it or rent from a company that doesn't charge for additional drivers. If your spouse will be a second driver, rent from a company that allows both a husband and wife to drive at no extra cost.
- When you reserve a car, always ask for a confirmation number. When you pick up your car, verify the discount or special rate *before* signing the agreement and ask if a better rate has become available since you booked.
- When you call to ask about rates or reservations, always be armed with your organization's ID number and your own membership card for reference. Present them again at the rental counter when you pick up your car, and be sure to confirm your rate before signing the agreement.
- Don't purchase insurance you don't need. Review your personal auto insurance coverage and credit-card policy to determine if you require the optional loss/damage coverage offered by the rental companies. Your homeowner policy may cover your personal belongings on the road.
- If you are traveling outside the U.S., don't wait until you arrive at your destination to arrange a rental and, if applicable, discuss your age. Book your car here before you go because renting abroad is much more expensive. Remember to request your senior discount. Consult with your insurance carrier and credit-card companies to be sure you are covered overseas. Most personal automobile insurance covers you only for driving in the U.S., and coverage may not include certain types of vehicles.

■ If you can drive a stick shift, you can cut the cost of a rental significantly. In other countries, automatic transmissions are not readily available and when they are, they are much more expensive.

ADVANTAGE RENT-A-CAR

This agency's new Senior Advantage program is offered exclusively to drivers age 50 or better, charging just $25 a day for economy through full-size cars and $35 a day for minivans or small SUVs. The special rate is available at participating U.S. locations, subject to availability and possible blackout dates, and requires 24-hour advance reservation. Request the rate code ADMSCS.

For information: 800-777-5500; www.advantage.com/seniors.

ALAMO RENT A CAR

For people over 50 who belong to AARP, Alamo takes up to 25 percent off the standard daily, weekly, or monthly leisure rates at more than 1,000 locations in the U.S. and Canada. *For information:* 800-GO-ALAMO (800-462-5266) or 800-786-3064; www.alamo.com.

AUTO EUROPE

If you rent a car from Auto Europe—a company that services more than 4,000 car-rental locations worldwide—you are guaranteed the lowest rates based on those of comparable car-rental companies. And, if you are 50 or over, you will also get a discount of 5 percent, sometimes even on top of sale rates, on all rentals, including chauffeur drives and prestige sports cars.

Short-term leases are also available from Auto Europe, which has partnered with Peugeot to lease factory-new cars for periods of more than 17 days. All short-term leases include unlimited mileage; insurance; 24-hour, English-speaking roadside assistance; and taxes. And, very important to many travelers, unlike car rentals that may be limited to drivers between the ages of 25 and 70, there is no maximum age requirement.

For information: 888-223-5555; www.autoeurope.com.

AVIS RENT A CAR

Check out Avis's special rates for members of AARP before snapping up any other special deals. You're entitled to discounts of 5 to 25 percent off the lowest rate from this company with more than 4,600 agencies in 160 countries, plus unlimited mileage at participating locations. Check the website for coupons that may save you more money.

For information: 800-331-1800; www.avis.com.

BUDGET RENT A CAR

Budget gives members of AARP 10 percent off the regular daily, weekly, or monthly rates; 5 to 20 percent off some promotional rates; and unlimited mileage at participating locations. In addition, it makes some special money-saving offers from time to time.

For information: 800-527-0700; www.budget.com or www .budget.com/aarp.

ENTERPRISE RENT-A-CAR

Enterprise, the largest car-rental agency in North America, specializes in renting vehicles in residential and commercial neighborhoods. That means its 7,000 or so locations world-wide are in big cities and small towns as well as at major airports. It offers 5 percent off the standard daily, weekly, and monthly rental rates to members of AARP.

For information: 800-RENT-A-CAR (800-736-8222); www.enterprise.com.

EUROPE BY CAR

Europe by Car offers short-term leases of factory-new Peugeots and Renaults for periods of at least 17 days. All leases include collision and theft insurance with no deductible, unlimited kilometers, and 24-hour emergency assistance. If you are a member of AARP, you'll get a flat rate discount depending on the type of car and the duration of your lease. There's no upper age limit for drivers.

On car rentals, you'll also get a 5 percent discount, unlimited mileage, and all of the other perks.

For information: 800-223-1516 or 212-581-3040; www.europebycar.com.

HERTZ CAR RENTAL

Members of AARP are eligible for savings at participating Hertz locations all over the world, with discounts of 5 to 25 percent off the leisure rates. Included are unlimited mileage, enhanced insurance coverage, and periodic bonuses such as upgrades and savings coupons.

For information: 800-654-2200; www.hertz.com.

KEMWEL

This car-rental broker, with multiple suppliers, offers a discount of 5 percent off any rental including sale rates to anybody over the age of 50 at any of its locations in Europe. Ask for it when you make your booking whether by telephone or online. Kemwel also offers short-term leases that are valid for a minimum of 17 days and a maximum of 264 days on brand-new Peugeots, complete with nondeductible, fully comprehensive insurance; 24-hour roadside assistance; and unlimited mileage. Best of all, there is no maximum age limit for drivers.

For information: 800-678-0678; www.kemwel.com.

NATIONAL CAR RENTAL

National's deal with AARP gives you 5 to 20 percent off the regular leisure rates at participating locations, plus unlimited mileage. As usual, see if you can get a better rate, and, if you can't, go with this one.

For information: 800-CAR-RENT (800-227-7368); www .nationalcar.com.

RENAULT EURODRIVE

As an alternative to car rentals, Renault Eurodrive offers short-term leases valid to drive in more than 43 countries for a minimum of 21 days and a maximum of five months. For leisure travelers who live outside Europe, the program provides a new tax-free, factory-new, fuel-efficient Renault vehicle with unlimited mileage; comprehensive insurance coverage with no deductible; an extensive service network; and access to 24-hour, English-speaking road assistance. The 35 pick-up and drop-off sites are located in nine European countries, so you may pick up your car in one location and leave it in another.

Customers are charged a set fee for the first 21 days and a nominal fee per day for the remaining time. Although leasing may be cheaper in the long run than car rentals, even more important to many travelers is the fact that there is no maximum age requirement, whereas car rentals are often limited to drivers between the ages of 25 and 70.

For information: 800-221-1052 or 212-730-0676; www .renaultusa.com.

RENT-A-WRECK

This company, whose cars are not wrecks but three to five years old, claims to be 15 to 20 percent cheaper than the major car-rental agencies. Because all of its 250 locations across the country are independently owned, it is up to each one of them to set its own senior discount, but most give renters who are at least 50 or 55 years old a 5 to 10 percent discount off the regular rates. Cars are rented for round-trips only and must be returned to their home locations.

For information: 800-944-7501; www.rentawreck.com.

7

Saving a Bundle on Trains, Buses, and Boats in North America

Getting around town, especially in a city where driving is not a practical option, probably means depending on public transportation to get you from hither to yon. Remember that once you reach a particular birthday—in most cases, your 60th or 65th—you can take advantage of some good senior markdowns on trains, buses, and subways. All you need in most cases is a Medicare card, a Senior ID card, or your driver's license to play this game, which usually reduces fares by half. Although you may find it uncomfortable at first to pull out that card and flash it at the bus driver or ticket agent, it soon becomes very easy. Do it and you'll realize some nice savings.

And don't fail to take advantage of the bargains available to seniors on long-distance rail, bus, and boat travel as well.

RIDING THE RAILS

Just about every commuter railroad and metropolitan transit system in the U.S. and Canada gives older passengers a break on fares, although you may have to do your traveling during off-peak periods when the trains are not filled with go-getters rushing to and from their offices. New York's Metro North, for example, charges anyone over 65 only half the regular fare for all trains except those arriving in Manhattan during weekday morning peak hours. On the New York subways and buses, you pay only half whether you pay with cash, tokens, or a Reduced Fare MetroCard. In Chicago too the fare is half price. In Washington, D.C., passengers who are 65 or more pay only 60 cents instead of $1.25 to ride the buses and half fare on Metrorail trains. Pennsylvania and Illinois let you ride for free. See Chapter 16 for local transportation bargains.

As for serious long-distance journeys, many mature travelers are addicted to the railroads, finding riding the rails a leisurely, relaxed, romantic, comfortable, economical, and satisfying way to make miles while enjoying the scenery.

So many passes and discounts on railroads are available to travelers heading for other parts of the country that sorting them out becomes confusing. But, once you do, they will help stretch your dollars while you cover a lot of ground.

See Chapter 8 for the best deals on transportation in foreign countries for travelers of a certain age.

ALASKA RAILROAD

Passengers over 65 are entitled to a 20 percent reduction on winter fares from October until May aboard the Aurora Winter Train and the Hurricane Train between Anchorage and Fairbanks and anywhere else in between. You're encouraged to take food and drink with you because there's limited food service on the train for this 12-hour journey.

For information: 800-544-0552; www.alaskarailroad.com.

AMTRAK

For the growing numbers of senior travelers who love to travel by rail, Amtrak offers those 62 or over a 15 percent discount on most trains, including Explore America Fares, in the U.S. and on some Canadian routes, every day of the week. The discount is also available on Saturdays and Sundays on the Acela Express and Metroliner Service but not on weekday Acela Express, the Auto Train, or sleeping accommodations.

Amtrak and Via Rail Canada have teamed up to offer the North America Rail Pass. It lets you travel to more than 900 destinations, with unlimited stopovers on the 28,000-mile rail system in the U.S. and Canada, for 30 consecutive days after the first day of use and you must travel in both countries. If you're at least 60, you are entitled to 10 percent off the regular adult fare. You can buy the pass, good during peak and off-peak seasons, from either company or a travel agent. You'll need advance reservations and you'll travel coach, although you may upgrade to business class or sleeping accommodations for an additional charge.

If you are over 50 but haven't yet reached the age of 60 or 62 to qualify for the privileges described here, and you *are* a U.S. military veteran, you can get the same 15 percent—occasionally even more—if you join Veterans Advantage, a service organization, for $59.95 a year. The discount applies on most trains throughout the U.S. A three-day advance purchase is required.

For information: 800-USA-RAIL (800-872-7245); www .amtrak.com. For Veterans Advantage: 866-838-7392; www .veteransadvantage.com.

ONTARIO NORTHLAND

This passenger railroad serving northeastern Ontario gives travelers over the age of 60 a 10 percent fare reduction any day of the year on the Northlander train running between Toronto and Cochrane and stations in between. For round-trips on the same route, the Senior Excursion Return Fare is an even better deal, giving passengers over 60 a 20 percent discount on Tuesdays, Wednesdays, and Thursdays. On the Polar Bear Express that runs between Cochrane and Moosonee, the reduction for seniors is 10 percent.

For information: 800-461-8558 or 705-472-4500; www .northlander.ca.

VIA RAIL CANADA

The national Canadian railroad, which provides coast-to-coast passenger service, gives seniors 60-plus a 10 percent discount off the full economy-class adult fare every day of the year, even on top of other special fares. Most of the time it is a good deal, but sometimes a better one for all ages may be offered, so always ask for the best available fare.

Via Rail's Senior Bring a Friend for Free Fare is another perk for the 60-and-over set. For every ticket in Comfort (economy) class at the regular senior fare, a companion travels free. In Sleeper and first class, a companion gets 75 percent off the regular fare. You must request the companion fare when you book your tickets. You may also board the train early, again if you ask for the privilege when you make your reservations.

At 60 you are also eligible to buy three economy-class rail passes at a 10 percent discount. The first is the Canrailpass, available for peak or off-peak travel and valid for 12 days within a 30-day period anywhere on Via Rail's transcontinental system. You may get on and off the train as many times as you wish, stopping wherever you like along the way, after reserving your space for all segments.

The second pass to offer a 10 percent senior discount is the Corridorpass. Sold year-round for first-class or economyclass seating, it gives you ten days of unlimited train travel within the Quebec City–Windsor corridor.

And last, the North America Rail Pass, a cooperative venture with Amtrak, allows you to explore North America by train, giving access to all Via Rail trains in Canada and almost all Amtrak trains in the U.S. at a 10 percent discount. It gives you 30 consecutive days of unlimited travel to about 900 destinations in the U.S. and Canada. You get as many stopovers as you like but no more than four one-way trips on any given route or segment. Reservations are required for the entire journey, and you must travel in both countries to use this pass.

For information: 888-VIA-RAIL (888-842-7245); www .viarail.ca.

GOING BY BUS

Never, never board a bus without asking the driver whether there's a senior discount, because even the smallest bus lines in the tiniest communities (and the largest—New York City, for example) in the U.S., Canada, and abroad give seniors a break, usually 50 percent off at age 60 or 65. In Europe, your senior rail pass is often valid on major motorcoach lines as well, so always be sure to inquire.

COACH CANADA

This bus line, with first-class scheduled routes between many cities in southwest Ontario and Quebec, offers discounts of 10 percent and sometimes more to passengers over the age of 60.

For information: Coach Canada, 791 Webber Ave., Peterborough, ON K9J 7B1; 800-461-7661 or 705-748-6411; www.coachcanada.com.

GRAY LINE WORLDWIDE

Gray Line is an association of about 150 independent sightseeing tour companies on six continents. Participating locations give members of AARP a discount of 10 percent on fares for half- or full-day sightseeing tours. You must purchase tickets at a Gray Line terminal and present a valid membership card. Some Gray Line companies also give discounts to nonmembers if they are 55 or 60, so inquire before signing up for a tour.

For information: Call the Gray Line Worldwide office in your area or the corporate headquarters at 303-394-6920; www.grayline.com.

GREYHOUND CANADA

Here you'll get 10 percent off all regular fares, any day of the week, year-round, if you are over 62 with a valid ID.

ALASKA MARINE HIGHWAY SYSTEM

Traveling in the off-season on the Alaska Marine Highway System (AMHS)—also known as the Alaska Ferry, and the only maritime "road" in the country—in the off-season is a bargain for foot passengers 65 and older. Between October and April, you sail for half the regular adult fare. The discount does not apply to vehicle or cabin space or a round-trip on the same sailing to the Aleutian Islands. Sometimes in the summer, too, there are half fares for seniors on several of the smaller vessels. The message is always ask if a senior rate is available.

For information: 800-642-0066; www.dot.state.ak.us/amhs.

What's more, if you're traveling with a companion and buy your tickets five days in advance, your companion pays only $20 one way or $40 round-trip.

For information: 800-661-8747; www.greyhound.ca.

GREYHOUND LINES

The largest intercity transportation company, Greyhound gives passengers over 62 a 5 percent discount on any non-discounted fare.

For information: Call your local Greyhound reservation office or 800-231-2222; www.greyhound.com.

ONTARIO NORTHLAND

On all Ontario Northland's scheduled intercity bus lines in northeastern Ontario, passengers over the age of 60 are offered a 10 percent discount on the regular fare every day of the week. On round-trips on Tuesdays, Wednesdays, and

Thursdays, the Senior Excursion Return Fare is an even better deal, giving passengers over 60 a 20 percent discount.
For information: 800-461-8558 or 705-472-4500; www .ontarionorthlander.ca or www.webusit.com.

PETER PAN BUS LINES

All passengers 62 or over can get a 5 percent discount on the nondiscounted fare on some routes aboard Peter Pan buses and Bonanza Bus Lines. Peter Pan is concentrated mainly in the Northeast.
For information: 800-343-9999; www.peterpanbus.com.

8

Cutting Your Costs Abroad

he most enthusiastic voyagers of all age groups, Americans over 50 spend more time and money on travel than anybody else, especially when it comes to going to foreign destinations. It's been estimated that more than four out of every ten passport holders are at least 55 years old. And there's hardly a country in the world today that doesn't actively encourage mature travelers to come for a visit.

Because you are now being avidly pursued, you can take advantage of many good deals in other lands. Although foreign airlines are not as generous as they used to be, railroad and bus systems in most European countries give seniors deep discounts that are especially valuable if you plan an extended stay in one place. Even ferries and cruise ships are often ready to make you a deal. This chapter gives you a rundown on these and other ways to cut your overseas holiday costs, especially if you are planning a trip on your own. For the U.S. and Canada, see Chapter 7.

But, first, keep in mind:

- Always ask about senior savings when you travel on planes, trains, buses, or boats anywhere in the world. Do the same when you buy tickets for movies, theaters, museums, tours, sightseeing tours, historic buildings, and attractions. Don't assume, simply because you haven't heard about them or the ticket agent hasn't mentioned them, that they don't exist. Senior discounts are becoming more and more common everywhere, and you'll be amazed how much money you can save.
- Some countries require that you purchase a senior card to take advantage of senior discounts, but most require only proof of age, usually in the form of a passport.
- Always have the necessary identification with you and be ready to show it. Occasionally you may need an extra passport photograph.
- You must purchase most European rail passes in the U.S. or Canada at least 15 days before your departure. However, some national passes that are good only within one country's borders are not available here and must be purchased there, usually at major railroad stations or airports. Have your passport handy. It's best to check out all your options before you make your plans. Don't buy a pass unless you know you'd spend at least the same amount on individual tickets.
- Although there are many European rail pass plans, only a few of them offer senior discounts to travelers age 60 or over.

- Be sure your rail pass is validated at a railway ticket office the first time you use it, before boarding the train.
- Ask about rail pass insurance when you buy your pass, just in case it is lost or stolen during your trip. You might want to seriously consider overall travel insurance as well.
- Major U.S. hotel chains, such as Radisson, Marriott, Choice, and Best Western, offer senior discounts that almost always apply at their participating properties in other countries.
- Travel passes for sightseeing trips are available in confusing profusion, and because many overlap and some must be purchased before you leave home, it's wise to check them out before you go. Contact the national tourist offices of the countries you plan to visit.
- Tourist passes usually cost older travelers the same as everyone else, but in most cases they are definitely worth buying. Among the best buys everywhere are the inexpensive, easy-to-use "city cards" available for many major European cities. Usually good for one to four days, they give you free public transportation plus admission to the most important tourist sites and, frequently, discounts on tours, meals, theater tickets, cultural attractions, and shopping.

EUROPE BY RAIL

If you intend to pack a lot of train travel in Europe into your stay, rail passes can make the going cheaper and easier, especially if you travel with a companion or a group. Some passes are multinational, valid in more than one country.

Others cover transportation within the borders of one country only. Many passes must be purchased here before you leave and are not available overseas, while others may be purchased only in the country that issues them, so it is extremely important to explore the possibilities well in advance of your departure. Always ask if there is a senior discount on the pass you want. Some passes give seniors a break, others don't. Just remember that some any-age options can be better choices than the senior deals.

Most rail passes are available in two versions: the *flexipass* permits travel for a specified number of days within a certain time period (such as any 4 days in one month); the *consecutive-day pass* is valid on any day within a certain period of time (such as 15 days in a row). Whichever you choose, you must have it validated at a railway station ticket office before you board the train the first time you use it.

If you're not going to pile up the miles in a relatively few days, however, you may be better off buying individual train tickets with a senior discount. All you need to qualify as a senior in many countries is your passport or other ID that proves you are at least 60 or 65. However, in the U.K. you may want to buy a British Senior Railcard, which gives you a third off on almost any ticket. In Germany consider a BahnCard or in France a Carte Senior, good for a 25 percent discount on all rail tickets and up to 50 percent on many off-peak trips. Check it all out in this chapter.

EURAIL PASSES

A group of 37 railways and shipping lines, Eurail markets rail passes that will take you everywhere in Europe. In fact,

FINDING A DOCTOR OVERSEAS

Before you leave on a trip to foreign lands, you would be wise to send for the **International Association for Medical Assistance to Traveller's** (IAMAT's) list of physicians all over the world who speak English, have had medical training in North America or Europe, and have agreed to reasonable preset fees. When you join the free, nonprofit IAMAT, you will get a membership card entitling you to its fixed rates, a directory of English-speaking physicians in 125 countries and territories, and advice on immunizations and preventive measures for many diseases, including malaria.

For information: IAMAT, 1623 Military Rd., Niagara Falls, NY 14304; 716-754-4883; www.iamat.org.

it issues so many passes that it's not easy to decide which one you need. But here is an overview.

The traditional Eurailpass is valid for unlimited first-class train travel on all the major railways and some shipping lines of 18 European countries for periods of 15 days to three months. The Eurailpass Flexi provides 10 or 15 travel days in first class within a two-month period. The Eurailpass Saver for two or more people traveling together saves 15 percent per person. None of these passes is discounted for seniors, but all are definitely worth considering if you plan to cover many miles across many borders, especially since they also entitle you to free or discounted travel on many buses, ferries, steamers, and suburban trains.

Another option, the Eurail Selectpass, the most popular pass because of its flexibility, lets you choose three, four, or five adjoining countries that are connected by train or ship and get unlimited first-class passage for 5 to 15 days, consecutive or not, within a period of two months.

All of these rail passes must be purchased *before* leaving on your European holiday as they are not sold over there. And remember that none of them give seniors a special break. Buy them from a travel agent or directly through the following agents.

For information: Eurail Group, www.eurail.com. Rail Europe, 800-438-7245; www.raileurope.com. DER Destination Europe, 800-782-2424; www.DER.com. ACP Rail International, 866-9-EURAIL (866-938-7245).

EUROSTAR

The Channel Tunnel train, connecting London with Paris or Brussels, makes many round-trips a day beneath the English Channel. You're eligible at age 60 for the senior fares that are about 40 percent cheaper than the regular adult fares on both first-class and standard tickets. The tickets are unrestricted and refundable, but because there is a limited number of discounted seats available on each train, it's smart to book well in advance. If you have a rail pass, ask about the passholder fare that might save you even more than the senior fare.

For information: Rail Europe, 800-438-7245; www.rail europe.com. Eurostar, 800-EUROSTAR (800-387-6782).

THALYS TRAIN

Thalys, the European high-speed rail network, with trains that connect Paris with Brussels, Cologne, Deüsseldorf, and Amsterdam, gives a discount of more than 30 percent on the cost of first- and second-class tickets to travelers 60 and older. Tickets may be booked three months in advance.

For information: Rail Europe, 800-438-7245; www.rail europe.com.

MULTICOUNTRY RAIL PASS
BALKAN FLEXIPASS SENIOR

A discounted pass for travelers 60 or older, the Balkan Flexipass Senior lets you roam by train through Bulgaria, Greece, Macedonia, Montenegro, Romania, Serbia, and Turkey. The first-class pass, good for 5, 10, or 15 days within a one-month period, costs about 20 percent less than the equivalent regular adult pass and includes the same bonuses, such as special prices on ferry crossings, cruises, and hotels.

For information: Rail Europe, 800-438-7245; www.rail europe.com.

COUNTRY-BY-COUNTRY TRAVEL DEALS
AUSTRIA

Women who are at least 60 and men at least 65 can purchase an official Senior Citizen Railway card for about $30 and travel around Austria at half fare on all trains and buses run by the federal government. That makes it a good deal if you are planning many journeys within this country. You can get it at major rail stations in Austria.

On its nonstop service across the Atlantic to 130 destinations in 66 countries, Austrian Airlines gives a discount of 10 percent to passengers over 62 and a younger companion on some published nonsale fares.

The Vienna Card and similar city cards in other Austrian cities and provinces, including Salzburg, Linz, and Innsbruck, are very good buys. Sold for varied numbers of days, they give you unlimited travel on all public transportation—no more fumbling for the proper change—as well as free or reduced admission to museums, shops, attractions, and historic sites.

For information: Austrian National Tourist Office, PO Box 1142, New York, NY 10108; 212-944-6880; www .austriatourism.com.

BELGIUM

If you are a 65-plus visitor to Belgium, you may travel between any two railroad stations within the country on Belgian Rail trains for the bargain rate of 4 euros. You must travel second class and return on the same day. Departures on weekdays must be after 9 A.M. On weekends and public holidays (except during the high tourist season or on a few major holidays), the deal is on all day.

Something else to remember is that most hotels in Brussels offer a big reduction on room rates on weekends and during July and August when the staffs of many of the international organizations based there leave town for vacation.

For information: Belgian National Tourist Office, 220 E. 42 St., New York, NY 10017; 212-758-8130; www.belgium .com. For Belgian Railways: www.sncb.be.

BRITAIN

Bargains abound in the U.K., undoubtedly the most popular foreign destination for Americans. Senior rates and special privileges are offered almost everywhere, from railroads and bus lines to museums, theaters, swimming pools, and historic sites. Visitors over 60, for example, get good breaks on the cost of admission to Windsor Castle, Hampton Court, the Tower of London, Kensington Palace, Westminster Abbey, St. Paul's Cathedral, Kew Gardens, and many more favorite visitor destinations. So be sure to carry proof of age with you, although you won't need it at many London museums, such as the British Museum and Tate Modern, because everyone regardless of age now gets in free.

Mature theatergoers in London can buy tickets last-minute at half price or sometimes less at most major theaters simply by arriving at the box office after 6 P.M. for evening performances and about an hour before the curtain rises for matinees. Have your ID in hand and ask for "Senior Standbys."

Also, don't forget that Marriott, Choice, Best Western, and other international hotel chains offer their senior privileges at most of their locations around the world, including the U.K. That means you can get a senior discount on the room rate almost everywhere you go.

For information: Visit Britain, 551 Fifth Ave., New York, NY 10176; 800-462-2748; www.visitbritain.com/usa.

Traveling by train. In Britain, where virtually every town can be reached by train, it often pays to buy a rail card or rail pass that can make your travel cheaper. For example, the British Senior Railcard, available to anyone at least 60, can save you a third off the cost of a regular adult fare. It currently costs 24 pounds and is valid for a year. It's good on most tickets, first class or standard, including promotions and excursions, throughout Britain, except on journeys made wholly within the London and South East area, or during morning peak periods on weekdays. You can buy it at British Rail mainline stations.

Another way to save on train travel if you're 60 or more is to buy a multiday first-class BritRail Pass. It comes in several varieties, all of which cost you 15 percent less than the regular first-class adult fares, although they cost more than the regular adult second-class passes. They are not sold in the U.K., so you must get yours before your departure. They cannot be used in Ireland or on special excursion trains, but they do include service between London and its three international airports, Heathrow, Gatwick, and Stansted. With your pass, you may get on and off as often as you like.

Your first choice is the BritRail Senior Flexipass, sold for 4, 8, or 15 days (consecutive or not), that allows unlimited travel in England, Scotland, or Wales over a period of two months. Travelers over 60 get a 15 percent discount on first-class tickets.

The second option is the BritRail Consecutive Senior Pass that gives you unlimited train travel anywhere you want to go within the same three countries but must be used on consecutive days. This version is sold for 4, 8, 15, 22 days or a month, first class only. It too costs 15 percent less than the regular adult pass.

Then, for those over 60 who want to travel first class only within England, there is a choice of the BritRail England Senior FlexiPass and the BritRail England Consecutive Senior Pass, both available for varying numbers of days of first-class travel.

With any of the rail passes, request the "family pass" if you are going to be traveling with children. For no extra cost, it allows one child age 5 through 15 to go free with each adult pass holder. Additional children 5 through 15 ride at half fare, and those under 5 are free.

By the way, if you're 60-plus and purchase a BritRail package with both air and accommodations from ACP Rail, you're entitled to an ACP Secrets discount of 5 percent.
For information: BritRail, 866-BRITRAIL (866-274-8724); www.britrail.com. ACP Rail, 866-9-EURAIL (866-938-7245); www.eurail-acprail.com. Rail Europe, 800-438-7245; www .raileurope.com.

Sightseeing passes. The **Scottish Explorer Pass** gives you unlimited admission to 75 of Scotland's top historic properties, including castles, abbeys, and distilleries. What's more, at age 60 you are entitled to the "concession" discount of about a third off the regular price.
For information: Buy it at Tourist Information Centers or Historic Scotland properties; or www.historic-scotland .gov.uk.

Other sightseeing passes include the Great British Heritage Pass, the Britain Card, the London Visitor Travelcard, the London Pass, and the Welsh Historic Monuments Explorer Pass. All very useful but none of these is discounted for seniors.

Traveling by bus. At 60, you can ride for up to half price on most National Express coaches that go to about 1,000 destinations in England, Scotland, and Wales. Ask for the "routesixty fares" when you buy your tickets.
For information: www.nationalexpress.com.

In Scotland, the Scottish Citylink offers senior specials that change periodically. Recent senior specials saved 60-plus passengers 50 percent on coach travel between Edinburgh and Glasgow or between Aberdeen and Dundee. Check out the possibilities when you buy tickets at Citylink ticket offices.

For information: www.citylink.co.uk.

DENMARK

Many of Denmark's state-run museums, such as the National Museum, are now free to everyone every day; others are free to all visitors on select days, usually Wednesdays; and most other museums give a break to seniors.

When you buy tickets for the Danish State Railway system at any train station in Denmark, be sure to ask for the discount for passengers 65 and older. You get a 50 percent reduction on tickets every day, except Friday and Sunday and some holidays when the discount drops to 25 percent.

The Color Line ferries with several international routes linking ports in Denmark, Norway, Germany, and Sweden charge passengers who are 60 or more and their younger travel companions only half fare, except on some routes in midsummer and on holiday weekends.

When traveling by air, remember that SAS offers passengers over the age of 62 a 10 percent discount on some flights from North America to Scandinavia and other destinations in Europe, but only on the highest fares, making them useful only when you must fly at the last minute.

To make things easier and cheaper, be sure to buy a Copenhagen Card. Available at tourist information centers in the city, it is valid for 24, 48, or 72 hours of free or discounted admission to the major sights in and around town, plus unlimited free travel on all buses and trains in the metropolitan area.

For information: Danish Tourist Board, 655 Third Ave., New York, NY 10017; 212-885-9700; www.visitdenmark .com.

FINLAND

Travel within Finland is discounted, sometimes steeply, for people 65 or over. Simply show proof of your age—your passport—at the ticket office, and you will get a 30 percent reduction on train tickets as well as motorcoach journeys covering at least 80 kilometers one way.

Although the Helsinki Card is not discounted by age, it offers substantial savings on a city tour and admission to museums, exhibitions, attractions, buses, trams, and metro

HEALTH COVERAGE ABROAD

The standard Medicare plan, with a few exceptions, does not cover medical or hospital costs outside the U.S. Some Medicare HMOs do cover emergency procedures abroad but not routine care, and many of the available Medigap policies provide 80 percent, after a deductible, of the cost of emergency care incurred in the first two months of a trip outside the country. If you do not carry your own private health insurance that will pay the expenses incurred overseas, talk to your travel agent about temporary health insurance that will cover you for the length of your trip.

For information: Call 800-MEDICARE (800-633-4227); www .medicare.gov.

and commuter trains within the city limits. Available at the airport, many hotels, and tourist offices, it is sold for periods of one, two, or three days.

For information: Finnish Tourist Board, 655 Third Ave., New York, NY 10017; 212-885-9700; www.gofinland.org.

FRANCE

Wherever you go in France, from museums to historic sites, movies and theaters to concerts, always ask whether there is a senior discount and you will be amazed how often you'll get one. Most Paris municipal museums, by the way, are free to everyone.

The privileges that come with age are especially good, however, when it comes to transportation. You are offered several choices. For example, simply by showing proof that you are 60 or more when you buy a ticket at a railway station, you will get the Decouverte Senior rate that gives you 25 percent off on all TGV rail services (except overnight accommodations) in first or second class throughout the entire country, except on trips in peak hours entirely within the Paris Transport Region. You will get the same reduction on non-TGV mainline and regional rail services for travel during off-peak periods on tickets purchased at the train station.

If you plan to travel extensively in France, you may prefer a Carte Senior, which costs about EUR 50 and is sold at railroad stations. Valid for a year, again at age 60, it allows unlimited travel in first or second class at a 50 percent discount on some journeys, except in the Paris area during peak hours and a 25 percent discount on others, including trains that connect France with other European countries.

This card requires a passport photo when you buy it at a major train station or through a travel agency. It may *not* be used from 3 P.M. Sunday to noon Monday, or noon Friday to noon Saturday.

For information about the Decouverte Senior rate and the Carte Senior: www.tgv.com.

Finally, there is the France Seniorpass, exactly the same as the France Pass, but a little cheaper to buy for travelers who are 60-plus. Both must be purchased on this side of the Atlantic before departure. The Seniorpass gives you any three days of unlimited first-class travel within a month and the option of buying up to six additional rail days. Bonuses include discounts on river cruises, hotels, Eurostar, and Thalys trains, Paris attractions, and scenic railways, as well as reduced rates to some museums.

For getting around in Paris, the Paris Visite Card, available for varying numbers of days, allows you unlimited travel anywhere in the city on public transportation. That includes the metro, buses (including shuttle buses to central Paris from the airports), the RER (fast trains between main stations), the tramway, the Montmartre Funicular, and all SNCF trains in the greater Paris region. You may buy it here or in Paris at metro or SNCF stations and tourist offices.

And here's something else. Seniors are invited, along with the disabled and families with small children, to ride the elevator to the top of the Arc de Triomphe for a panoramic view of the city.

For information: French Government Tourist Office, 825 Third Ave., New York, NY 10022; 212-838-7800; www .franceguide.com.

GERMANY

Many restaurants in Germany have a *Seniorenteller*, a special menu that offers lighter fare in smaller portions at a lower cost for older guests. Ask to see it and also ask if there are discounts for seniors wherever you go. You'll find they are available in places such as department stores, hair salons, museums, and historic sites, and for other attractions such as day cruises on the Rhine. Even some hotels and spa resorts have them, especially in off-peak seasons.

If you plan to settle down in Germany for a month or more, intend to cover many miles by train, and are over 60, you may want to buy a BahnCard 50 Senior for first-class travel at any railway station (have your passport and an extra photo with you). The card, valid for a year, costs you half the regular adult pass and gives you 50 percent off on tickets anywhere in Germany on Deutsche Bahn. For a small additional fee, you can get a BahnCard Rail Plus that takes 25 percent off the regular adult fares on the foreign portions of train trips from or to Germany. The cards are available only in Germany.

For those who would rather travel by motorcoach, Deutsche Touring, a long-distance bus line that will transport you in comfort almost anywhere in Germany as well as to most other European countries, takes 10 percent off the price of all tickets for all passengers 60 or older. You can buy tickets through a travel agent, at DER travel agencies, on the Internet, or at railroad stations.

Lufthansa, the official German airline, will give you a 10 percent discount on transatlantic flights if you're over 60 but only on the highest unrestricted fares, so it's not a practical choice unless you're flying at the last minute.

Finally, check out the city cards, available at local tourist offices, railway stations, and hotels in most major cities, for savings on transportation, tours, and admissions.

For information: German National Tourist Office, 122 E. 42nd St., New York, NY 10168; 800-651-7010 or 212-661-7200; www.cometogermany.com. Deutsche Touring, www.touring.de. Rail Europe, 800-438-7245; www.raileurope.com.

HONG KONG

In this bustling city, there are several ways to save money on transportation, assuming you are at least 65. The *Star Ferry* will take you free of charge on the eight-minute crossing from central Hong Kong to Kowloon, giving you a fabulous view of Victoria Harbor. You pay half fare on the Mass Transit Railway (MTR), the HYF Ferry to outlying islands, the Light Rail (LR), and the Kowloon-to-Canton Railway (KCRC). And on the famous Peak Tram, you are offered a discount of about 60 percent off the regular adult fare. Always be prepared with an ID, such as your passport.

Several museums, too, give seniors age 60 or more a break on admissions, charging only half the regular entrance fee.

The Cultural Kaleidoscope program in Hong Kong schedules free events several times a week to introduce visitors to English-speaking specialists who share their knowledge of local traditions. Among the topics are tai chi, the rituals of tea, an architecture walk, Cantonese opera, Chinese medicine, and even a ride on a Chinese junk. Pick up a brochure at a visitor information center.

For information: Hong Kong Tourist Board, 800-282-4582 or 212-421-3382; www.discoverhongkong.com/usa.

IRELAND

Going by rail in Ireland is an easy and relaxed way to see the country. If you're planning to cover a lot of territory, consider buying the Ireland Senior Pass good for any five days of second-class travel within a period of one month. At age 60 and beyond, you're entitled to a nice discount off the regular second-class adult cost. Remember to have the pass validated before starting your first journey.

For information: ACP Rail, 866-9-EURAIL (866-938-7245); www.eurail-acprail.com. BritRail, 866-BRITRAIL (866-274-8724); www.britrail.com. Rail Europe, 800-438-7245; www.raileurope.com.

JAPAN

To get around Japan on its fast and spotless railroads, there is no better deal than the Japan Rail Pass, although it offers no special senior privileges. It is available only to visitors to the country and allows unlimited travel on almost all Japan Railway trains and its affiliated bus and ferry lines for 7, 14, or 21 days.

Before you leave home, you must buy an exchange order for your Japan Rail Pass from an authorized travel agent in North America (a list of authorized agents in your area is available from the Japan National Tourist Organization). When you get to Japan, you must trade the exchange order for the pass at any JR Travel Service Center in international airports and major railroad stations. Passes for regional travel are also available, some of which may be purchased here and others only in Japan. Check with your travel agent.

By the way, if you are going to take domestic flights among cities in Japan, buy your tickets here before you go, so you'll be entitled to the One World Yokoso/Visit Japan Fares or the Welcome to Japan Fares that are offered only to foreign visitors. You will pay less than you would if you waited until you arrived there. Also, you can take advantage of discounted travel on almost all services on the JR Transportation Network, including the bullet train.

Although Japan Airlines no longer offers senior discounts, special low fares are often available through some Japanese travel agencies. Ask about them at the Japanese National Tourist Organization.

Two special programs are especially appealing to older visitors to Japan and are designed to make your trip more enjoyable. Welcome Cards, for example, are available in many cities or areas of the country, giving you discounts and special services at art galleries, museums, sightseeing attractions, shops, restaurants, and transportation. Pick them up at tourist offices.

The Good Will Guide System (SGG) connects foreign travelers with local volunteers in 63 cities or towns who offer free private guided tours. Brochures with details about the program are available at the Japan National Tourist office or on its website.

For information: Japan National Tourist Organization, 1 Rockefeller Plaza, New York, NY 10020; 212-757-5641; www.japantravelinfo.com. Japan Railways, 212-332-8686; www.japanrail.com.

NEW ZEALAND

Starting at age 55, you qualify for a savings of 30 percent off the full standard fares on Tranz Scenic's train journeys throughout the country. Tickets for travel on the country's only passenger railroad are not sold here but must be purchased once you've arrived in New Zealand.

The Interislander, the ferry that sails between the North and South Islands of New Zealand, gives a discount of up to 25 percent to travelers who are 60-plus.

You can take a sightseeing tour with Newman's Coach Lines or a bus trip to any of 600 towns and cities all over the country on InterCity Coachlines and get the Golden Age Fare available to anyone, resident or visitor, over the age of 60. You'll pay about 20 percent less than the standard adult fare.

Many museums and other major tourist attractions in New Zealand offer seniors substantial discounts, so remember to ask when you buy your tickets.

For information: Tourism New Zealand, 501 Santa Monica Blvd., Santa Monica, CA 90401; 866-639-9325; www.new zealand.com. For the Seniors Card: www.seniorscard.co.nz. For Tranz Scenic: www.tranzscenic.co.nz.

NORWAY

In this beautiful country, you're entitled to half fare on buses and trains, anytime, anyplace. For this break, however, you must be at least 67 and ready to prove your age with a proper ID. Younger spouses traveling with you get the same privilege.

You can save money—50 percent—when you travel on the Color Line's ferries on six international routes linking seven ports in Norway, Denmark, Germany, and Sweden. The reduced rate is valid all year for passengers who are 60-plus and an accompanying companion, except on some routes in midsummer and on weekends.

SAS, the Scandinavian airline, offers travelers 62 or over a 10 percent discount on most flights to Scandinavia and its other international destinations, but only on the highest fares so you're better off without it unless you must travel at the last minute.

And check out the Norway Fjord Pass (www.fjord pass.com). It costs about $10 and offers discounts on rooms in hotels, guest houses, apartments, and holiday cottages.

As you should everywhere, ask if there is a senior discount wherever you go and consider purchasing city cards for Oslo and Bergen. They will provide free public transportation plus free or discounted admission at most museums, historic sites, and cultural attractions.

For information: Innovation Norway Tourism, 655 Third Ave., New York, NY 10017; 212-885-9700; www.visitnorway .com/us.

PORTUGAL

If you're over 65, you're entitled to a senior discount almost everywhere you go in Portugal. For example, you pay only half price to ride the railroads and get a reduction of 15 percent on express buses just by showing the ticket agent proof of your age. The same goes for the 29 museums operated by the Portuguese Institute of Museums where you pay only 50 percent of the usual adult fee for admission.

At age 55, you can be a guest at most of Portugal's famous pousadas for much less than the regular rate (except in peak travel periods) by taking advantage of the Golden Days Program that gives you a 40 percent discount per night per room and includes breakfast for two. The pousadas are the historic government-owned inns throughout the country, many of them in converted castles, convents, or palaces, and all of them charming. The special rates are valid every day, with some exceptions mainly during major holiday periods. There is a surcharge on Friday and Saturday nights. Only one guest per double room must be 55.

Another good deal is the Lisbon Card, sold for periods of 24, 48, or 72 hours and good for free admission to museums and monuments, discounted admission to other major attractions, and free access to public transportation on the city's buses, trams, undergrounds, lifts, and trains to Sintra and Cascais. You can buy the card at tourism offices.

For information: Portuguese Trade and Tourism Office, 590 Fifth Ave., New York, NY 10036; 212-354-4403; www.visit portugal.com. For pousadas: Pousadas de Portugal; www .pousadasportugal.com.

ROMANIA

Unlimited travel on the national rail network of Romania is what you get with a Eurail Romania Pass Senior, which is valid for any five or ten days within a two-month period and will cost you, if you are at least 60, about 20 percent less than the regular pass for younger people. It also allows for savings at several hotels.

For information: Eurail Group, www.eurail.com. Rail Europe, 800-438-7245; www.raileurope.com.

SPAIN

In addition to discounts for mature travelers at just about every museum, cultural event, and historic site in Spain, there is another good deal for visitors over 60. The Golden Days Promotion offers a 30 percent discount on the official rate for a room and breakfast at most of the country's famous paradores. These are government-owned inns, 91 of them, many of them converted palaces, castles, and convents, scattered throughout the country. The special senior rates apply all year although there are blackouts in some popular months of the year. You must request the Golden Days rate when you make your reservations. There is only a certain number of rooms available at the special rate, so make those reservations as early as you can. Only one guest sharing a room must be 60.

For information: Tourist Office of Spain, 666 Fifth Ave., New York, NY 10103; 212-265-8822; www.okspain.org. For paradores: www.paradores-spain.com. Or www.paradoresof spain.

SWEDEN

Travel by bus in Sweden is inexpensive and hassle free. Besides, seniors get substantial discounts. Hop on a local bus in Sweden, and, if you're 65, you'll pay about 40 percent less than the regular fare. Travel on the express buses operated by Swebus Express, the country's largest long-distance bus operator with 300 destinations in Sweden, and you are offered a 30 percent discount starting at age 60.

For seeing the sights in the greater Stockholm area, consider buying the SL Tourist Card sold at tourist offices and kiosks. It's half price for seniors (about $12 for three days). With this card, you get free transportation on buses, local trains, subways, and ferry tours.

When you travel on the Color Line's six international ferry routes linking seven ports in Norway, Denmark, Sweden, and Germany, you pay only 50 percent of the standard adult fare if you are 60 or more and an accompanying companion gets the same deal. There are some blackouts on some routes in midsummer and weekends when the half-price fare is not available, so try to be flexible.

SAS, the Scandinavian airline, still offers a 10 percent senior discount to transatlantic passengers over 62 on flights originating in the U.S., but only on the most expensive full fares. However, on domestic flights within Sweden, you can often find special fares if you're over 65.

And don't forget the city cards—the Stockholm Card, Gothenburg Card, and Malmo Card. These very good deals give you free or discounted transportation and admission to places you'll want to visit.

For information: Swedish Travel and Tourism Council, 655 Third Ave., New York, NY 10017; 212-885-9700; www.visit-sweden.com.

SWITZERLAND

The Swiss Museum Passport is valid for an entire month of unlimited visits to about 240 museums. If you are a woman over 62 or a man over 65, you may buy it at a discount at participating museums and tourist offices in Switzerland.

Swiss International Air Lines gives a 10 percent discount to passengers 62 or older and to a travel companion, but only on the highest unrestricted fares across the Atlantic. So unless you must travel at the last minute or require extreme flexibility, forget it. You can surely find a lower fare available to all ages.

For information: Switzerland Tourism, 608 Fifth Ave., New York, NY 10020; 877-794-8037 or 212-757-5944; www.my switzerland.com.

9

Trips and Tours for the Mature Traveler

Many enterprising organizations, tour operators, and travel agencies now cater exclusively to the mature traveler. They choose destinations designed to appeal to those who might have already "been there and done that," arrange trips that are leisurely and unhassled, give you congenial contemporaries to travel with and group hosts to smooth the way, and provide many special services you never got before. They also give you a choice between strenuous action-filled tours and those that are more relaxed.

Options range from cruises in the Caribbean or the Greek Isles to grand tours of the Orient, sightseeing excursions in the U.S., trips to the Canadian Rockies, theater tours of London, safaris in Africa, and snorkeling vacations on the Great Barrier Reef of Australia. There's no place in the world where mature travelers won't go.

There are many choices, too, for the growing number of intrepid, energetic, and courageous members of the 50-plus population who prefer travel that is adventurous and unusual, perhaps even exotic. Many are described in this chapter along with the more traditional variety. Because they are planned specifically for the seasoned traveler, they usually offer some measure of comfort and convenience even in the wilderness, plus a leisurely pace that allows time for relaxation and independent exploration. Most important, they offer clean, comfortable accommodations, though sometimes rustic or spartan, and almost surely a private bathroom.

AFC TOURS AND CRUISES

Specializing in escorted tours designed for mature travelers, AFC schedules all-inclusive trips to all the most popular destinations in the U.S. and Canada and some in other countries. Not only that, but if you live in southern California, Phoenix, or Las Vegas, you will be transported free between your home and the airport. Many of the most popular tours are "unpack once," which means you stay in one hotel and take day trips from there. Domestic tours take you to such places as the national parks, Branson, Charleston, New York City, Savannah, the Pacific Northwest, and Washington, D.C. International adventures cover much of Europe plus Australia and New Zealand. Other choices are cruises, steamboating, train tours, and holiday tours. In other words, almost anything you want.

Singles: if you sign up for the Sharefinder Service four months in advance and a roommate cannot be found to share your room, you need not pay a single supplement.

For information: AFC Tours and Cruises, 11772 Sorrento Valley Rd., San Diego, CA 92121; 800-369-3693 or 858-481-8188; www.afctours.com.

CIE TOURS INTERNATIONAL

An agency specializing in escorted vacations in Ireland, Northern Ireland, Scotland, Wales, and England, as well as to Italy and other European destinations, CIE offers motor-coach tours and fly/drive vacations, some of which come with a "55 and Smiling Discount." This means that on certain departure dates for several escorted vacations you get $75 per person off the cost of the trip if you are 55 or older and are among the first 15 people to join the tour.

For information: CIE Tours International, 10 Park Pl. SW, PO Box 1965, Morristown, NJ 07962; 800-243-8687 or 973-292-3438; www.cietours.com.

COLLETTE VACATIONS

Collette Vacations has been around for more than 80 years, offering worry-free worldwide vacations to the mature traveler. Its escorted tours move at a relaxed pace, put you up in good hotels, and provide experienced tour guides to see that all goes well. But this agency offers other kinds of vacations too. For example, its "hub and spoke" programs feature multiple nights in one place—city stays, resort stays, castle stays—so you can settle down for a while without constantly climbing on buses and unpacking your bags at the next destination. Meanwhile, day excursions take you to see the sights.

Collette's independent travel packages, land-only or air-inclusive, let you customize your own trip in North America or Europe. You have hotel options at each destination, optional activities, and rental cars or train transportation if you want them.

Something of interest to many senior travelers: Collette's cancellation waiver policy, which you can buy, allows you to cancel your trip for any reason up to the day of departure for a full cash refund.

Members of AARP are offered savings on many Collette trips.

For information: Collette Vacations, 162 Middle St., Pawtucket, RI 02860; 800-340-5158 or 401-727-9000; www.collette vacations.com.

ELDERHOSTEL

The educational tours from Elderhostel number in the thousands, many of them bargains for adults over the age of 55 and younger travel mates. See Chapter 13.

For information: Elderhostel, 11 Avenue de Lafayette, Boston, MA 02111; 877-426-8056 or 617-426-7788; www .elderhostel.com.

ELDERTREKS

The first adventure travel company to specialize in exotic, far-out adventures for travelers 50 and over (and companions over 18), ElderTreks takes small groups of no more than 16 participants to more than 50 destinations worldwide, from Argentina to Mongolia, Pategonia, and Tibet. Designed for people who enjoy physical activity, its programs are rated from easy to challenging. Itineraries, however, are chosen with older trekkers in mind, so if you are in good condition, you'll fit right in. On ship-based adventures, the expedition ships are small to allow for more personal interaction and less impact on the environment.

Hotels are selected for comfort, location, charm, and availability of private washrooms. Accommodations in primitive places may be the floor of a nomadic tent or beneath a canopy of trees, but you can always count on a mattress. Guides, cooks, meals, and porters are part of the package.

There is no additional charge for single travelers willing to share a room.

For information: ElderTreks, 597 Markham St., Toronto, ON M6G 2L7; 800-741-7956 or 416-588-5000; www.elder treks.com.

FANCY-FREE HOLIDAYS

Geared for senior travelers, Fancy-Free's domestic escorted motorcoach tours, all originating in Chicago, include the usual favorite destinations such as Branson, New England, Alaska, Williamsburg, Asheville, New Orleans, and Washington, D.C. Its fully escorted overseas tours by air, motorcoach, or cruise ship include Ireland, England, Scotland, and Wales. If you live in the Chicago area, you'll be picked up at your home for free.

For information: Fancy-Free Holidays, 24 W. 500 Maple Ave., Naperville, IL 60540; 800-421-3330 or 630-778-7010; www.fancyfreeholidays.com.

FESTIVE HOLIDAYS

Another agency that caters to the 50-plus crowd, this one offers tours for organized groups of 40 participants to everywhere from Myrtle Beach, Nashville, Maine, Chicago, Quebec City, and New York to the national parks, Las Vegas, Europe, South Africa, and Australia—plus plenty of cruises. All packages are escorted and include accommodations, meals, and just about everything else.

In addition, Festive Holidays offers an innovation called "drive-to tours" for individual travelers, allowing them to take advantage of group discounts that make the trips remarkably inexpensive. On these, mostly to beaches on the East Coast, you drive yourself to your destination—for example, Ocean City, Myrtle Beach, Cape Cod, Lake George, Niagara Falls—and join others traveling on their own for meals, entertainment, and tours.

For information: Festive Holidays, 5501 New Jersey Ave., Wildwood Crest, NJ 08260; 800-257-8920 or 609-522-6316; www.festiveholidays.com.

50PLUS EXPEDITIONS

If you're an active traveler who's 50 or more and yearns for adventure in exotic destinations, consider these "Adventure Travel for People Over 50" tours that range from explorations of the rain forest in Ecuador to cruises in Antarctica, cycling in the Czech Republic, hiking in Borneo, or riding elephants in India. All are graded easy, moderate, or demanding, based on the level of physical activity each day and other factors such as elevation and climate. Limited to 16 participants, the tours are all-inclusive and put you up in comfortable accommodations with private facilities. In fact, however exotic, everything is planned for your comfort.

For information: 50plus Expeditions, 760 Lawrence Ave. West, Toronto, ON M6A 3E7; 866-318-5050 or 416-749-5150; www.50plusexpeditions.com.

GLOBAL ED-VENTURES

Based in Australia, Global Ed-Ventures features trips, independent and escorted, created specifically for active adults over 50. Most of its destinations are in exotic settings in Australia, New Zealand, Southeast Asia, and even Mongolia. All come with educational prereading material and detailed preparatory information so you know how you'll be faring wherever you're going. Its adventurous, cultural, and heritage journeys include 19 nights in Vietnam and Cambodia, 21 days camping in Australia's tropical northwest area, 5 days in North Queensland bordered by the Coral Sea Islands and the Great Barrier Reef, 18 nights exploring Mongolia's little-known areas including the Gobi Desert. You'll be treated to informative talks and lectures and travel in groups of no more than 32 people, all around your age.

For information: Global Ed-Ventures, Springboard Vacations, 6033 W. Century Blvd., Los Angeles, CA 90045; 866-447-7746 or 310-242-9234; www.globaledventures.travel/springboard.

GLOBUS AND COSMOS TOURS

This affiliated pair of tour companies, Globus and Cosmos, together the largest in the world, specializes in escorted travel to 65 countries on six continents, all designed to appeal to over-50 travelers who constitute the majority of its clientele. Globus offers upscale first-class tours while Cosmos specializes in escorted vacations for more cost-conscious travelers. Among their many varieties of travel styles are fast-paced multi-country tours and regional vacations that allow time to get the flavor of a specific place. Globus's LeisureStyle Vacations include more leisure time, two or three nights in each city, and cultural activities. Independent Vacations provide flexible itineraries at one's own pace with advice and assistance from an on-site host. Some trips combine cruises with land tours, others are river cruises all over the world, while specialty vacations include family vacations, religious explorations, and driving packages.

For information: Globus & Cosmos Tours, 5301 S. Federal Circle, Littleton, CO 80123; 866-755-6581 or 303-797-2800; www.globusandcosmos.com.

GO AHEAD VACATIONS

Go Ahead Vacations specializes in educational escorted sightseeing trips. It caters to the 50-plus traveler with international tours that include everything from airfare to guided sightseeing, the entire journey accompanied by full-time local tour directors so you can experience the places you visit from the perspective of a native.

In addition to its escorted tours, Go Ahead also features walking tours and combination land and cruise tours, as well as independent city-stay vacations that let you linger in one city for as long as you like, all with pre- and posttour extension options.

For information: Go Ahead Vacations, 1 Education St., Cambridge MA 02141; 800-599-1170 or 617-619-1000; www.goaheadvacations.com.

GOLDEN AGE TRAVELLERS CLUB

An over-50 club that specializes in discounted cruises on major lines everywhere in the world, Golden Age also offers a few land tours from well-known tour operators. When you join the club ($10 single or $15 per couple a year), you receive a newsletter with listings of upcoming sailings. Check

NEWS FOR 50-PLUS TRAVELERS

A couple of lively newsletters are dedicated to keeping 50-plus travelers up to the minute on what's available, exciting, and designed especially for them. *The Over-50 Thrifty Traveler* focuses on wandering the world on a small budget and describes deals, strategies, and resources that will save you money, stress, and hassles. Its sister publication, *The Over-50 Luxury Traveler*, concentrates on where and how to spend time and money in all the places the rich and famous go, but tells you how to do it less expensively

A third newsletter, *ThriftyTraveling.com*, is designed for all ages but includes a special section for over-50 travelers that will give you tips on saving money and finding new adventures. Other sections concern solo travel, traveling with children, cruise news, hotel deals, Internet news and more.

Each of these bimonthly, 10-page newsletters is available online or by mail for $29.95 per year.

For information: ThriftyTraveling.com, Inc., PO Box 1499, Port Richey, FL 34673; 800-532-5731; www.over50traveling.com.

the website for senior cruise specials of the week. For members in the San Francisco and Sacramento areas, there are one-day travel shows where you may meet fellow travelers and share a snack.

For information: Golden Age Travellers Club, 4302 Redwood Hwy, San Rafael, CA 94903; 800-258-8880; www.gat club.com.

GRAND CIRCLE TRAVEL

Grand Circle Travel, the first U.S. company to market international vacations for Americans 50 and over, is celebrating its 50th anniversary this year. It still caters to the older traveler average age 73, and plans all of its affordable trips exclusively for them. That means the trips are easygoing with longer overall stays, unhurried itineraries, and plenty of time to relax.

Grand Circle specializes in four varieties of travel. Its classic and educational escorted tours take groups of mature travelers all over the world, accompanied by experienced guides who take care of everything. All you have to do is show up and keep your eyes open.

Its extended-stay vacations allow you to travel in a group but, at the same time, be an independent traveler. You stay up to two weeks in one, two, or three destinations such as the Costa del Sol, Sicily, or Thailand. You live in hotels or apartments, with meals, social activities, tours, and a program director included.

River cruises are another option, taking you on leisurely voyages aboard the company's own fleet of ships, including private river boats, canal barges, and chartered yachts and motor cruisers. And finally, the ocean cruise tours combine sailing the major seas with land-based stays for in-depth explorations of the ports of call.

All vacations offer pre- and posttrip extensions that allow travelers to see more while taking advantage of their already included airfare.

If you are a solo traveler, you may ask to be matched with an appropriate roommate to avoid the single supplement or choose a trip or certain departure dates when the supplement is waived.

Bonus: organize a group of ten friends and relatives to travel with you on a GCT trip, and you go free.

For a free booklet, "Going Abroad: 101-Plus Tips for Mature Travelers," call Grand Circle Travel's 800 number below. *For information:* Grand Circle Travel, 347 Congress St., Boston, MA 02210; 800-248-3737 or 617-350-7500; www .gct.com.

GRAND EUROPEAN TOURS

Specializing in leisurely high-end, soft-adventure escorted tours for senior travelers, Grand European Tours believes that most of us don't enjoy rushing from place to place and living out of a suitcase. So it provides minimum stays of two to four nights in every overnight location on its trips to Europe, the Mediterranean, Australia, New Zealand, and Mexico. Even more relaxed options are the "super leisure" tours that give you four nights or more in each place, so you can rest and rejuvenate while exploring the world.

Hotels are first-class, travel is by motorcoach, tour directors accompany the group, local guides show you the sights, and the "explore and discover" program provides hands-on cultural experiences. Air and almost everything else is included in the price. An inexpensive protection policy allows you to change your travel plans for any reason up to 48 hours before the scheduled departure and get full credit for future travel.

For information: Grand European Tours, 6000 Meadows Rd., Lake Oswego, OR 97035; 800-552-5545 or 503-718-2262; www.getours.com.

HORIZON & CO.

Luxury adventures are what this company calls its trips to destinations that range from desert palaces to the Canadian wilderness, a bird sanctuary in India, or the meandering tributaries of the Mekong Delta.

Horizon & Co. divides its adventures into two categories, each designed to appeal to a different segment of mature travelers. The first, its Classic Series, is primarily for 65-plus travelers who want an all-inclusive, meticulously organized, small-group tour that provides safety and security while covering as much ground as possible at a comfortably relaxed pace.

On the other hand, its Exploratory Series, which may be escorted or independent, is for the younger, more active grownup traveler who is looking for unusual experiences; luxury; serendipity; small, intimate, upscale accommodations; and sophisticated cuisine.

For information: Horizon & Co., 478 Queen St. East, Toronto, ON M5A 1T7; 800-387-2977 or 416-585-9911; www.horizon-co.com.

MAYFLOWER TOURS

Most of Mayflower's travelers are "55 or better," so the pace of its tours is leisurely and rest stops are scheduled every couple of hours. On most tours, you travel by motorcoach, stay in good hotels or motels, and eat many of your meals together. Or choose a rail tour for spectacular scenery and adventure. All trips are fully escorted by tour directors who make sure all goes well. If you are a single traveler and request a roommate at least 30 days before departure, you'll get one or a room to yourself with no single supplement to pay. Tours go almost everywhere in the U.S., Canada, and the rest of the world, especially Italy, Greece, Australia, and New Zealand.

For information: Mayflower Tours, 1225 Warren Ave., Downers Grove, IL 60515; 800-323-7604 or 630-435-8500; www.mayflowertours.com.

NATURAL OUTINGS LTD.

This family-owned, Canadian soft-adventure travel company specializes in affordable small-group hiking trips in North and Central America and Europe, hiking remote footpaths and less-traveled roads suited to 50+ hikers, and staying in small hotels, jungle ecolodges, and mountain cabins. On its trips, you stay in comfortable lodgings and set forth every day to hike on easy terrain at an unhurried pace to see new sights and get acquainted with the local populace.

For information: Natural Outings LTD., PO Box 1000, Erin, ON N0B 1T0; 800-668-8911 or 519-927-3916; www.natural outings.com.

ODYSSEYS UNLIMITED

Small-group travel is this company's specialty. The philosophy here is that tours and cruises for grownups should allow for a leisurely pace, spontaneity, and flexibility, making its array of choices a good fit "for people who are accustomed to independent travel" but no longer want to be bothered with the details. Trips are limited to 12 to 24 participants, the cost covers everything from air to gratuities, and overnight stops let you stay put in one place for at least two nights and sometimes as many as five. Trips go to places all over the world, including Morocco, South Africa, Sicily and southern Italy, Eastern Europe, Vietnam, and plenty more.

For information: Odysseys Unlimited, 2 Newton Pl., 255 Washington St., Newton, MA 02458; 888-370-6765 or 617-454-9100; www.odysseys-unlimited.com.

OVERSEAS ADVENTURE TRAVEL (OAT)

A sister company to Grand Circle Travel but catering to a younger group, OAT plans soft adventures, exclusively for active travelers over 50, that combine creature comforts with off-the-beaten-path experiences all over the world, from China, Europe, the rain forests of Borneo to Botswana, the Amazon and a Red Sea cruise that stops in Egypt, Sinai, Jordan, and Saudi Arabia. Its three new 50-passenger ships sail along the Dalmatian Coast as well as in the Red Sea.

Groups are small, with no more than 16 participants. The trips—rated from easy to demanding—move at a leisurely pace and offer many optional side adventures. You'll travel by minivan and lodge in accommodations ranging from five-star hotels to jungle lodges or spacious tents and sometimes use unconventional modes of transportation such as dugout canoes, camels, yachts, or your own two feet.

Solo travelers are not charged a single supplement if they are willing to share accommodations.

Bonus: get ten of your friends and relatives to travel with you on an OAT trip, and you go free.

For information: Overseas Adventure Travel, 247 Congress St., Boston, MA 02210; 800-955-1925 or 617-350-7500; www.oattravel.com.

RIVER ODYSSEYS WEST (ROW)

ROW reserves a few rafting, fishing, and canoeing trips in every summer exclusively for adventurous people over 50 who like to travel with others their own age. These five-day prime-time trips take you down Montana's scenic upper Missouri River, on flat water following the trail of Lewis and Clark in a comfortable 34-foot voyageur canoe that carries up to 14 passengers and two guides. You'll stop for the night at luxury campsites at the edge of the river to eat five-course meals and sleep in big, comfortable tents.

For information: River Odysseys West, PO Box 579-UD, Coeur d'Alene, ID 83816; 800-451-6034 or 208-765-0841; www.rowadventures.com.

SENIOR TOURS CANADA

Canada's largest operator of escorted tours for the mature traveler, this company takes 50-plus tourists all over the world on leisurely vacations that range from tours of southern Italy to Florida spa holidays; Polynesian cruises; grand tours of Arizona, Antarctica, South Africa, or Japan; and stay-put holidays in Turkey, Portugal, or Palm Springs. You can choose among traditional tours, stay-put vacations, cruises, and bus tours. All are escorted and include everything from airfare to meals, gratuities, luggage handling, guided tours, and health and cancellation insurance. In other words, no hassle.

For information: Senior Tours Canada, 225 Eglinton Ave. West, Toronto M4R 1A9; 800-268-3492 or 416-322-1500; www.seniortours.ca.

SIERRA CLUB

The Sierra Club has created several summertime trips specifically for fit folks over the age of 50. The six-day trips are led by volunteers, and locations change every year. Recently, they have included backpack adventures in the Weminuche Wilderness in Colorado and the Wind River Range in Wyoming and hiking trips in Shenandoah National Park and Tahoe National Forest.

To participate, you must belong to the club. But if you're a senior, your yearly membership will cost you $25 instead of the usual $39. Two seniors in the same household pay $35 a year while the regular adult fee is $49.

For information: Sierra Club Outings, 85 Second St., San Francisco, CA 94105; 415-977-5500; www.sierraclub.org/outings/national.

TRAFALGAR TOURS

Trafalgar Tours has been catering to mature travelers for 60 years and offers hundreds of itineraries all over the world, each designed to be so hassle free, leisurely, and comfortable that guests, who needn't concern themselves with logistics and details, can relax and enjoy their travels. The fully escorted tours include luxury coaches, first-class or deluxe hotels or lodges, a tour director, guided sightseeing tours, and most meals. A major feature offered is a group of regional tours in the U.S. and Canada, while other trips go just about everywhere including Europe, Britain, New Zealand, and China. In addition, Trafalgar offers many choices of river cruising in Europe. If you are traveling alone, you may ask to be matched with a suitable roommate so that you can avoid the single supplement.

For information: Trafalgar Tours, 801 E. Katella Ave., Anaheim, CA 92805; 866-544-4434; www.trafalgar.com.

VANTAGE DELUXE WORLD TRAVEL

Vantage features upscale escorted group tours for mature travelers. These all-inclusive vacations include land tours all over the world, plus river and ocean cruises. Accommodations are always first-class or deluxe, and explorations are relaxed and include guided explorations and plenty of leisure time. Tour directors accompany you everywhere and take care of all the potential problems from ticketing and baggage handling to check-ins, meals, and tips. Among Vantage's most popular tours are a Danube River cruise, a trip through the Panama Canal, a visit to China and the Yangtze River, an exploration of Ireland, and a tour through the countries of Eastern Europe. There are also longer, more exotic trips, including a deluxe around-the-world tour.

If you are traveling alone and want a roommate, a compatible companion will be found or you'll pay only half the single supplement on escorted land programs. On river cruises, you are guaranteed a roommate or the per-person double-occupancy rate. On some departure dates, the single supplement is waived even without a roommate.

For information: Vantage Deluxe World Travel, 90 Canal St., Boston, MA 02114; 866-786-1989; www.vantagetravel.com.

WARREN RIVER EXPEDITIONS

Among the many whitewater rafting trips run by Warren River Expeditions, there are several just for adventurers over 50, plus two expeditions a year for grandparents and their grandchildren. All the trips take you down Idaho's Salmon

River, the longest undammed river in the country—fast and wild in the spring, tame and gentle in late summer. You'll float through unique ecosystems, down the deep Salmon River Canyon, and through the Frank Church Wilderness Area, where you'll view the lush scenery and abundant wildlife. Planned as soft adventure trips for people who are not enthusiastic about camping out, the six-day senior trips, limited to 16 guests, put you up each night in comfortable rustic backcountry lodges. There's a 10 percent discount on all trips for those over 55 and 25 percent for children 14 and under.

For information: Warren River Expeditions, PO Box 147, Carmen, ID 83462; 800-765-0421 or 208-756-6387; www .raftidaho.com.

WEST COAST RAIL TOURS

If you love to ride the rails, check out the tours run by West Coast Railway Association, a nonprofit society dedicated to the preservation of western Canada's railway heritage. The association restores, preserves, and maintains vintage railcars. Its unique excursions, one to nine days long, are escorted by experienced rail buffs and treat you to rail adventures in scenic and historic areas. On some tours, you eat and sleep on board; on others, you stop for meals and lodging along the way. Seniors, usually starting at age 60, get a price break on some of them.

For information: West Coast Rail Tours, PO Box 2790 Stn. Terminal, Vancouver, BC V6B 3X2; 800-722-1233 or 604-524-1011; www.westcoastrailtours.com.

10

Cruising the Oceans, Rivers, and Seas

Cruises have always appealed to the mature crowd. The majority of passengers on many sailings are over the age of 50, especially on longer voyages, and in fact, the longer the cruise, the older the passengers tend to be.

Whatever your age, never book a cruise without shopping around. Cruise rates have always been heavily discounted, but today anybody who pays the full sticker price (also called the brochure rate) should also be offered a chance to bid on that famous New York bridge. Usually the best bargains come from travel agents who specialize in sea voyages or from cruise brokers who buy blocks of cabins and sell them at a discount. But the cruise lines offer special rates, too, on advance-purchase or last-minute bookings, introductory or off-season sailings, repositioning cruises, group bookings, and two-for-one deals.

In your case, you should also see whether there are senior discounts, usually valid for age 55 and over, for the cruises that interest you. The easiest way to do this is to consult a travel agent or to check with a few cruise brokers such as www.vacationstogo.com (800-338-4962), www.mustcruise.com (888-516-6306), www.cruise411.com (800-553-7090), or www.ecruise.com (800-223-6868). Try using www.cruisecompete.com to compare costs. Cruise lines also offer special senior deals, especially on sailings that are not expected to sell out. Look for them on their websites, inquire by telephone, or ask your travel agent.

Sometimes seniors are offered other enticements such as free shore excursions, upgrades, and onboard credits. Make sure you're not missing something before you sign on.

By the way, some rates include port charges, taxes, and fees, and others don't. These can be substantial, so find out whether they have been included before comparing costs.

CARNIVAL CRUISE LINES

Carnival's occasional senior rates can save you up to $100 per person on some ships and departure dates if one occupant of the cabin is at least 55 years old. To find out about them, call your travel agent, a cruise broker, or the cruise line.

For information: 800-CARNIVAL (800-227-6482); www.carnival.com.

CELEBRITY CRUISES

This premium cruise line, whose nine ships make voyages to Bermuda, Alaska, Hawaii, Mexico, the Caribbean, Europe, and South America, features frequent senior specials for passengers 55 and over. Again, watch for them on the website, or ask your travel agent or cruise broker to check them out for you.

For information: 800-437-3111; www.celebrity.com.

ELDERHOSTEL'S ADVENTURES AFLOAT

One of Elderhostel's most popular categories of learning vacations for its 55-plus members is its selection of cruises on the world's most spectacular waterways. Your education will take place aboard river barges, yachts, cruise ships, or even a transatlantic ocean liner. Choices can be made from dozens of voyages all over the world, from the Mississippi River to Scandinavia, the Aegean Sea, the Yangtze River, the Texas Gulf Coast, the Danube River, and the Mediterranean. International programs include airfare, and all trips include tuition, field trips, meals, and accommodations. For more about Elderhostel, see Chapter 13.

For information: Elderhostel, 11 Avenue de Lafayette, Boston, MA 02111; 877-426-8056 or 617-426-7788; www.elderhostel.org.

FUN & FITNESS TRAVEL CLUB CRUISES

The aerobics cruises scheduled about once a month by this club for older adults take you on voyages in the Caribbean or along the Mexican Riviera, Australia and New Zealand, and the New England coast and Nova Scotia. Every morning, on every cruise, there are morning water aerobics led by certified instructors, plus other forms of physical activities such as yoga, tai chi, deck walking, ballroom dancing, and chair aerobics throughout the day, all exclusively for club members traveling together. The club, which costs nothing to join and is especially popular among single seniors, has a current enrollment of about 3,500 members nationwide.

For information: Fun & Fitness Travel Club, 7338 Dartford Dr., Ste. 9, McLean, VA 22102; 800-955-9942 or 703-827-1014; www.fun-fitness.com.

GRAND CIRCLE AND OAT CRUISES

The largest small-ship cruise line in the country, Grand Circle Travel's cruise division caters to older travelers who shun megaships and prefer smaller intimate vessels that can easily slip in and out of less-visited ports. With a fleet of more than 50 ships, including 16 river ships, five canal barges, three new 50-passenger ocean vessels, a 16-passenger expedition vessel, a 330-passenger oceangoing liner, and two dozen exclusive privately chartered yachts and motor cruisers, it serves two sister companies, Grand Circle Travel and Overseas Adventure Travel, both marketed exclusively to people 50 and over. Accompanied by trip leaders and local guides, passengers learn about the local culture onboard and off, dine on regional food, and glimpse everyday life and customs through intercultural activities.

For information: Grand Circle Travel, 247 Congress St., Boston, MA 02210; 800-248-3737 or 617-350-7500; www .gct.com.

HURTIGRUTEN

The Hurtigruten fleet (formerly known as Norwegian Coastal Voyage) sails daily year-round along Norway's 1,250-mile west coast, passing scores of fjords and calling at 34 ports between Bergen and Kirkenes above the Arctic Circle. Each ship plying the coast is a combination of a cruise ship that schedules shore excursions by foot, bus, or snow-mobile and a working ship that ferries local passengers and cargo between coastal villages. These unique cruise ships carry 312 to 675 passengers, and you may choose an escorted or independent vacation. Other expeditions include a world cruise and sailings to Antarctica or the Arctic and Greenland. If you are a member of AARP, you will be entitled to a savings of $100 to $150 per cabin, except in June or July, on many of these voyages.

For information: Hurtigruten, 800-323-7436 or 212-319-1300; www.hurtigruten.us.

NORWEGIAN CRUISE LINE

Every week, NCL offers new cruise specials including discounted fares for people 55 and up that usually amount to a savings of about 15 percent off the regular rates. You'll need a travel agent to find them for you.

For information: Norwegian Cruise Line, 800-327-7030; www.ncl.com.

OCEANIA CRUISES

Oceania caters specifically to the seasoned traveler who is looking for comfort, safety, "a country club flavor," smaller ships, longer itineraries, a lower price tag than the luxury lines, and plenty of amenities. Its ships carry 685 passengers on 10- to 35-day cruises that include more overnight port stays than any other line. They sail to Asia, South America, Europe, and Africa. Dress is casual, meals are open seating, and shore excursions may be customized.

For information: Oceania Cruises, 866-765-3630; www .oceaniacruises.com.

ROYAL CARIBBEAN INTERNATIONAL (RCI)

Check with your travel agent or the website to find out when this cruise line will be offering one of its periodic specials for passengers 55-plus and their cabin mates. They are available several times a year on all of its ships. And, so you know what you're getting into, each shore excursion on RCI voyages is rated mild, moderate, or strenuous.

For information: Royal Caribbean, 866-562-7625; www .royalcaribbean.com.

SAGA CRUISES

The voyages of the *Saga Rose* and the *Saga Ruby* are planned for travelers over 50 (and companions who may be as young as 40). Both of these small cruise ships that sail from English ports are owned by Saga Holidays, a British tour company that caters exclusively to mature travelers. They travel the world from the Mediterranean to the Baltic, the Caribbean, and even to the U.S. and Canada. Saga's newest ship, the *Spirit of Adventure*, much smaller, is even more port-intensive, offers longer itineraries, and sails to even more exotic destinations, including those along the Red Sea, the South China Sea, the Indian Ocean, the Mediterranean, and the Black Sea. As much time as possible is spent ashore to absorb the local flavor, while guest lecturers and experts fill you in on history and local culture.

For information: Yankee Holidays, 100 Cummings Center, Beverly, MA 01915; 978-867-1131; www.sagacruise.com.

GENTLEMEN HOSTS

Many cruise lines take a few gentlemen hosts along on their voyages to serve as dance partners and social hosts for single, older women passengers. The hosts are carefully selected unattached men age 40 to 70 who have impeccable manners, are good conversationalists, and have the ability to be charming no matter what. They must be excellent ballroom dancers, accomplished in everything from the rumba and the waltz to the fox-trot, cha-cha, rock and roll, and swing. They dance and socialize with the passengers for three or four hours every evening, host tables for dinner, attend parties and events, serve as partners in games, and help with shore excursions. They are, however, forbidden to get romantically involved with any of the guests. Hosts are unpaid volunteers who receive a virtually free cruise and, in fact, must usually pay a small fee for every day at sea.

Crystal Cruises, whose worldwide cruises carry four to six "ambassadors" per trip, look for personable men over the age of 65 who are great dancers and enjoy keeping older, single women passengers entertained both on board and ashore.
For information: Ambassador Host Coordinator, Entertainment Dept., Crystal Cruises, 2049 Century Park East, Ste. 1400, Los Angeles, CA 90067.

Cunard Cruise Line's voyages aboard the *Queen Victoria* carry along on all sailings six to ten friendly gentlemen hosts between the ages of 45 and 70. Their job is not only to whirl around the dance floor with women who need partners but also to act as friendly diplomats who help passengers get to know one another. A knowledge of foreign languages is a plus.
For information: Compass Speakers, 2455 E. Sunrise Blvd., Fort Lauderdale, FL 33304; 954-568-3801; www.compass speakers.com.

Cunard Cruise Lines also takes a couple of gentlemen hosts along on the *Queen Mary*'s voyages across the Atlantic. The host's job is to be charming, discreet, courteous, and a great dancer and conversationalist.
For information: Sixth Star Entertainment, 21 NW 5th St., Fort Lauderdale, FL 33301; 954-462-6760; www.sixthstar .com.

Holland America Line recruits single men with charm and great dancing skills for 14-day or longer cruises, transatlantic crossings, and big band sailings. Usually two to eight hosts go along on each trip.
For information: To Sea With Z, 19195 Mystic Pointe Dr., Aventura, FL 33180; 305-931-1026; www.toseawithz.com.

Majestic America Line sends at least two gentlemen hosts on most of its cruises aboard the *American Queen*, a 436-passenger riverboat, as it steams down the Mississippi River. The band plays music of the '40s and '50s, and the guests dance the night away.
For information: Compass Speakers, 2455 E. Sunrise Blvd., Fort Lauderdale, FL 33304; 954-568-3801; www.compass speakers.com.

Norwegian Cruise Line's sailings to many places around the world usually include at least two gentlemen hosts on longer voyages.
For information: To Sea With Z, 19195 Mystic Pointe Dr., Aventura, FL 33180; 305-931-1026; www.toseawithz.com.

Regent Seven Seas Cruises includes gentlemen hosts, chosen for their social skills and dancing talent, on most of the sailings on three of its vessels—*Seven Seas Voyager, Seven Seas Mariner,* and *Seven Seas Navigator.*
For information: Sixth Star Entertainment, 21 NW 5th St., Fort Lauderdale, FL 33301; 954-462-6760; www.sixthstar.com.

Silverseas Cruises has introduced a couple of Social Ambassadors on many longer trips aboard its luxurious small ships. The hosts' job is to dance, mingle, and mix, making sure all guests have an enjoyable voyage.

For information: Compass Speakers, 2455 E. Sunrise Blvd., Fort Lauderdale, FL 33304; 954-568-3801; www.compass speakers.com.

11

Intergenerational Adventures

I f you'd like to get to know your grandchildren (or children, nieces, nephews, young friends) better, take them on vacation. A trip with the kids or your adult children is a wonderful way to spend time together and share common interests, especially for far-flung families who seldom have a chance to enjoy one another's company. Whether it's a one-day tour of a nearby city or a week on a dude ranch, this is the kind of family togetherness that works. You can plan your own itineraries, maybe visiting places you both want to see, renting a cottage at the beach, or choosing a resort or cruise that offers special activities for the youngsters.

If you don't want the hassles and anxieties of traveling on your own with kids, you can do it the easy way by going with a tour company that specializes in intergenerational vacations. These are scheduled in the summer and during winter breaks when the children are out of school. The best of them are fully escorted by counselors, often schoolteachers on holiday. The tours, ranging from a visit to Washington, D.C., to a safari in Kenya, move at a leisurely pace suited to both generations with plenty of stops and time to relax and relate. Some are designed for children in a certain age range, while others accept all youngsters over 7 and up to 17 or 18.

By the way, consider taking a cruise together. Several cruise lines cater to children now, providing activities for all of them, from toddlers to teenagers. Besides, many ships have cabins that accommodate three or four passengers. These extra beds or bunks are often sold at very low rates, especially for children. And sometimes third and fourth passengers, children or otherwise, can go along absolutely free except for port taxes and extras.

Growing in popularity, too, are other multigenerational holidays such as adventures for mothers and grown daughters; parents and adult children; and whole families, including children, parents, and grandparents. If you're wondering why a growing number of organizations and companies and even hotels are now catering to grandparents, here's the reason. There are now about 60 million grandparents in the U.S., according to AARP, with the number expected to rise to 80 million by 2010. The average age for first-time grandparents is 48, giving them plenty of time and energy to spend with the kids.

ELDERHOSTEL INTERGENERATIONAL AND FAMILY PROGRAMS

Elderhostel's many multigenerational programs are designed to allow adults to participate in learning experiences with their younger relatives and friends. Its family offerings are open to the entire family and may include grandparents, aunts, uncles, adult children, and grandchildren. In any case, there is a limit of one child per adult. Usually the youngsters must be at least nine years old, and sometimes they must be within a specified age range. Many of the activities are for everyone together, while others are for the adults or the children.

You may choose programs in the U.S.—many in the national parks—or in foreign countries such as Bermuda, Costa Rica, Greece, New Zealand, Thailand, Mexico, and Nicaragua.

For information: Elderhostel, 11 Avenue de Lafayette, Boston, MA 02111; 877-426-8056 or 617-426-7788; www .elderhostel.org.

GENERATIONS TOURING COMPANY

With a wide array of upscale escorted tours for generations traveling together—some exclusively for grandparents and grandchildren, others for grandparents and/or parents and children—Generations Touring Company's goal is to create meaningful family connections and learning experiences for everyone. Each of its itineraries in the U.S. and other parts of the world from Mexico to Italy, Vietnam, Peru, and Antarctica is led by a travel manager, an educator-escort, and local guides. The tour price covers just about everything.

Certain departure dates are reserved for children ages 8 to 17, while others are limited to those 8 to 12 or 13 to 17. Trips are designated as GTC Journeys, which are not overly demanding, and GTC Adventures, designed for those who especially enjoy physical activities. On all trips each day includes a mix of experiences together and downtime when adults and children get their own space apart.

For information: Generations Touring Company, PO Box 20187, Seattle, WA 98102; 888-415-9100 or 206-325-2831; www.generationstouringcompany.com.

GRANDTRAVEL

The first company to send grandparents and their grand-children off on vacation together, Grandtravel continues to expand its list of intriguing trips for grandparents of any age and kids from 7 to 17. You needn't be an authentic grandparent, by the way—aunts, uncles, cousins, and other surrogate grandparents are welcome. The 5- to 15-day deluxe tours are all-inclusive, educational, and small, with a choice of destinations ranging from New York City to Kenya, South Africa, New Zealand, or Greece. They are led by teacher-escorts and include a multitude of activities for both age groups together as well as separately. Customized tours are a specialty too. Predeparture counseling is part of the package, designed to help you deal with special concerns such as what to pack or how to deal with kids who miss their moms.

For information: Grandtravel, 1920 N St. NW, Washington, DC 20036; 800-247-7651 or 202-785-8901; www.grandtrvl.com.

RASCALS IN PARADISE

Specializing in family vacations for parents and children, Rascals in Paradise also invites grandparents and grand-children, or everybody together, to go along on its adventure trips to places such as Mexico and the Caribbean, the Bahamas, Europe, New Zealand, Thailand, Australia, the Canadian Rockies, Africa, the Galapagos Islands, Hawaii, Alaska, and ranches in the West. All group trips, three to six families per group, include escorts who plan activities for the older children and arrange babysitters for the little ones. This agency will plan independent vacations, too, as well as family reunions and other multigenerational celebrations.

For information: Rascals in Paradise, 500 Sansome St., San Francisco, CA 94111; 800-872-7225 or 415-921-7000; www.rascalsinparadise.com.

RIVERBARGE EXCURSIONS

Aboard the 198-passenger riverboat *River Explorer*, the only hotel barge traveling America's inland waterways, you'll chug along on a four- to ten-day excursion exploring the country on its famous rivers. You'll stop along the way to visit nearby towns, eat home-style meals on board, and enjoy regional entertainment. Pricing is all-inclusive, including tips. Even better, you can take your grandchildren on one of the barge's Grand Vacations, scheduled year-round, that invite children 12 and under to sail free when sharing your stateroom and teenagers up to 18 to sail half price but in their own rooms.

By the way, if you are a teacher, active or retired, you can travel half price when you share a stateroom with someone paying full price.

For information: RiverBarge Excursion Lines, 201 Opelousas Ave., New Orleans, LA 70114; 888-GOBARGE (888-462-2743); www.riverbarge.com.

SAGAMORE GRANDS CAMP

Spend time, just you and the grandkids, at Grandparents and Grandchildren's Camps held in the summer at the Sagamore Conference Center, the Vanderbilt family's former summer retreat in the Adirondacks in New York State, and the oldest intergenerational program around. The Saga Grands Week, now sponsored in cooperation with Elderhostel and always booked far in advance, is from Sunday to Friday and is designed to foster connections between the generations and teach a respect for nature. Bring as many grandchildren ages 6 to 14 as you can handle—you'll be spending the whole day every day together.

For information: Great Camp Sagamore, PO Box 40, Raquette Lake, NY 13436; 315-354-5311; www.sagamore .org. For Elderhostel programs at Sagamore: 877-426-8056 or 617-426-7788; www.elderhostel.org.

SENIOR WOMEN'S TRAVEL (SWT)

Take your granddaughter(s) to Paris, or Venice and Florence, on a great adventure led by SWT. The grandmother/granddaughter trips are for just the two generations, no parents permitted, so you can spend a week together in the summer exploring the world and bonding. On the Paris trip, for example, you'll have private tours, a fashion show, a cooking demo, side trips to Versailles and Giverny, good food, and a studio apartment.

For information: SWT, 20 Van Winkle Rd., Hudson, NY 12534; 917-880-6732; www.poshnosh.com.

SIERRA CLUB

Among the famous outings of the Sierra Club, the largest grassroots environmental group in the country, are a few affordable summertime vacations for families and one just for grandparents and their grandchildren. This annual event is a six-day stay at the club's rustic Clair Tappan Lodge in Tahoe National Forest in California. The laid-back holiday is designed for people between the ages of 6 and 95 who may pick and choose among activities that include short hikes, fishing, lake swimming, a beach picnic, and a tram ride. Lodging and meals are part of the package.

To go, you must be a member of the club. If you consider yourself a senior, your yearly membership costs only $25, compared to $39 for other adults. Two seniors in the same household may join for $35 a year, compared to $49 for younger adults.

For information: Sierra Club Outing Dept., 85 Second St., San Francisco, CA 94105; 415-977-5500; www.outings .sierraclub.org/outings/national.

STRATHCONA PARK LODGE

With special programs in the wilderness for all manner of people, Strathcona Park Lodge includes intergenerational weeks throughout the summer for active grandparents and kids ages 9 through 14, one grandchild per grandparent. The lodge, located on Vancouver Island and surrounded by snowy peaks and dense forests, specializes in wilderness courses and outdoor adventures. Activities include canoeing and kayaking, orienteering, rock climbing, learning survival techniques, natural history discussions, and camping out. Accommodations are in lodges, timber chalets, or waterfront cottages. Buffet meals are included.

For information: Strathcona Park Lodge, PO Box 2160, Campbell River, BC V9W 5C5; 250-286-3122; www.strath cona.bc.ca.

TAUCK BRIDGES

Tauck's collection of vacations for families are scheduled in the summer months and during spring and winter breaks, when parents with children, grandparents with grandchildren, and families with multiple generations go off together to wonderful places. The escorted tours go everywhere from cowboy country in the American West to Alaska, Costa Rica, Italy, and Tanzania, and virtually everything is included in the price, making them worry-free adventures. The idea, of course, is to give families, many of whom live miles apart these days, a chance to bond with one another while having fun, learning new things, and exploring the world together.

For information: Tauck World Discovery, 10 Norden Pl., Norwalk, CT 06855; 800-788-7885; www.tauckbridges .com.

WARREN RIVER EXPEDITIONS

Take the grandkids down the Salmon River in Idaho on a raft trip run by Warren River Expeditions. On special summer trips reserved for grandparents and grandchildren, you'll float through canyons and forests, taking time to swim and kayak. You'll sleep in comfortable backcountry lodges, some quite rustic, along the river's edge and have plenty of exciting adventures on the big rubber rafts powered by expert oarspeople. At least two midsummer departures, with a 10 percent discount for those over 55 and 25 percent for children 14 and under, are reserved each summer for the two generations.

For information: Warren River Expeditions, PO Box 147 Carmen, ID 83462; 800-765-0421 or 208-756-6387; www .raftidaho.com.

12

Singles on the Road

If you're single, on your own again, have a partner who isn't the traveling kind and couldn't care less about seeing Venice, or simply like to travel independently, you can do it your way. Many people love to vacation without having to cater to anyone else's whims or demands about where to go, when to eat, how long to stay at the museum, or what time to go to bed. Others, however, find traveling solo to be a rather lonely business and would prefer not to wander around the world by themselves.

To encourage and accommodate the growing numbers of mature single travelers, many tour companies, cruise lines, and clubs cater to them. Some plan itineraries for the independents, while others organize singles group tours or schedule special departure dates specifically for solo travelers.

Most try to match singles up with roommates so they can avoid paying a single supplement, the extra charge for the privilege of sole occupancy of a room or cabin. If they can't manage to find a suitable roommate, they will usually reduce the supplement or even cancel it. Another way to avoid paying more than paired people is to book a tour with an agency that specializes in singles travel and offers a roommate-match guarantee. Or watch for special deals when single supplements are waived altogether. These are usually offered on off-peak packages with space that may otherwise go unclaimed.

Going with a group provides ready-made companions and an organized travel plan. But if you don't want to go places by yourself even in a group, consider joining a matchmaker club that helps you find a fellow traveler who is also looking for someone with whom to share adventures and expenses.

Finally, one of the surest ways to enjoy a vacation on your own is to sign up for a trip that features activities that you enjoy because you'll meet people who like the same things you do. Consider, for example, art tours, bike trips, golf schools, gourmet tours, tennis camps, language programs, or volunteer vacations.

TOURS AND CLUBS FOR SOLO TRAVELERS
ADVENTUREWOMEN

An early pioneer of adventure travel specifically for women, AdventureWomen was started in 1982 and schedules one- to three-week, small-group trips all over the world. Although it pitches its tours to women over 30, its typical participant is around 50 and many are a lot older, traveling alone or with friends, mothers, daughters, and sisters. The tours are adventurous, unusual, and physically active, and each is rated easy, moderate, or high energy, according to difficulty. Included among its many unusual vacations are hiking the Cinque Terre in Italy, exploring Bhutan, nature safaris in Costa Rica, touring Egypt and Jordan, and horseback riding in Ireland.

For information: AdventureWomen, 300 Running Horse Trail, Bozeman, MT 59715; 800-804-8686 or 406-587-3883; www.adventurewomen.com.

ALL SINGLES TRAVEL

Exclusively for the single traveler, All Singles Travel plans many trips a year for solos of all ages but schedules one or two specifically for those over 60 who prefer traveling with other people their own age. Many of its adventures are cruises, but there are land trips as well, such as tours to the Greek Islands, Iceland, the Rocky Mountains, and Costa Rica.

For information: All Singles Travel, 1 Glenlake Pky., Atlanta, GA 30328; 800-717-3231 or 770-645-3241; www.allsingles travel.com.

CONNECTING: SOLO TRAVEL NETWORK

Connecting, based in Canada, is an organization dedicated to helping its approximately 1,800 single members enjoy their travels, advising them where to go, what to do, and how to have a good time on a go-alone vacation. An online membership costs $35 per year or $50 for life for which

RVing WOMEN

Women travelers who take to the highways in recreational vehicles can get advice and support from RVing Women, a club with more than 2,200 members. The group sponsors rallies, caravans, and other events across the U.S., Canada, and Mexico, plus weekend RV maintenance and driving classes in many locations around the country. Members pay an annual fee of $45 ($55 the first year) and receive a bimonthly magazine that covers topics such as safety, scams on the road, vehicle maintenance, and announcements of upcoming events and an annual membership directory that puts you in touch with thousands of other women who may offer overnight space and hookups. Other benefits: educational programs and seminars, an annual convention, local chapters, and special discounts at businesses and campgrounds.

For information: RVing Women, PO Box 1940, Apache Junction, AZ 85217; 888-55-RVING (888-557-8464) or 480-671-6226; www.rvingwomen.com.

you'll get a 20-page electronic newsletter six times a year that includes destination reports, reader recommendations, a travel-companion exchange, listings of singles tours and cruises—some reserved for mature travelers—and helpful advice and tips. Another perk is the *Singles-Friendly Travel Directory* that lists hundreds of suppliers offering services or items of special interest to people who travel alone.

For information: Connecting: Solo Travel Network, 689 Park Rd., Gibsons, BC V0N 1V7; 800-557-1757 or 604-886-9099; www.cstn.org.

EXPLORATIONS IN TRAVEL

Women over 40 are invited to join this company's trips that combine adventure, physical activity, and culture. "Getting off the beaten track and being active outdoors" for a few days or more is the goal of these small-group tours led by women guides. Although there are overseas destinations such as the U.K. or Burma, most of the planned vacations take place right here in the U.S. and are designed to appeal to mature women who want to see the sights and get some exercise. For example, you can canoe on the Missouri River or the Rio Grande, hike in Virginia, and kayak in Vermont. *For information:* Explorations in Travel, 2458 River Rd., Guilford, VT 05301; 802-257-0152; www.exploretravel .com.

JUST US GIRLS TRAVEL

When you can't find the right person to travel with, you can join Just Us Girls Travel and be matched up with a travel partner: a woman who's also over 40 who wants your kind of trip and fits right in with your likes and dislikes on the road. Members fill out a lengthy questionnaire to detect personality traits and travel preferences and can post personal pages to give potential partners a chance to find out more about one another. Matched with one or more compatible travel mates, they take it from there, making their own contacts and decisions about traveling together. After a free trial period, membership costs $14.95 a month or $74.75 for six months.
For information: Just Us Girls Travel, 800-939-1910; www.just usgirlstravel.com.

O SOLO MIO SINGLES TOURS

A travel club for singles who like to vacation in groups, O Solo Mio welcomes people of all ages but most of its members are well over 50. An online newsletter announces upcoming plans and you may ask to be matched with a roommate to avoid paying a single supplement fee. The many tours and cruises vary every year, but recent destinations have included Vietnam and Cambodia, Kenya, Australia, Las Vegas, Chicago, and Italy.

For information: O Solo Mio Singles Tours, 160 Main St., Los Altos, CA 94022; 800-959-8568; www.osolomio.com.

SENIOR WOMEN'S TRAVEL

Senior Women's Travel is for "active and adventurous 50-plus women with a passion for travel." Its upscale, small-group guided tours concentrate on food, history, art, music, and literature. They take you to Paris, Venice, Rome, Barcelona, and Sicily, as well as plenty of other destinations.

Grandmother/grandchildren tours are recent additions. Adventures in Paris takes grandmothers and school-age granddaughters on whirlwind tours of Paris, Venice and Florence, San Francisco, or Boston during the summer vacation.

For information: SWT Tours, 20 Van Winkle Rd., Hudson, NY 12534; 917-880-6732; www.poshnosh.com.

SINGLES TRAVEL INTERNATIONAL

Mature active singles are the clients of this specialized travel agency that plans cruises and land vacations for both men and women who are traveling solo. Each trip includes get-togethers, tour options, parties, special events, and group dining. Recent adventures include a transatlantic dance cruise aboard the *Queen Mary 2*, an African safari, a trek in Peru, and a fiesta in San Antonio. If you want a roommate, you'll get one, or the single accommodations won't cost you extra. There's open seating for dining, making it easy to enjoy the company of the whole group.

For information: Singles Travel International, 877-765-6874; www.singlestravelinternational.com.

SINGLES TRAVEL SERVICE

You don't have to go it alone when there are tour operators like this one offering many different kinds of vacations, from cruises to escorted tours in China or Yosemite, ski trips, and summer camp. Most are for all ages, but some adventures each year are reserved for singles over the age of 40 so you can travel and party with people around your own age. A newsletter keeps you updated on what's coming next.

For information: Singles Travel Service, 1040 First Ave., New York, NY 10022; 212-752-2429; www.singlestravel service.com.

SINGLESCRUISE.COM

If you're a single and love to cruise, consider setting sail with a group of 100 to 400 solo travelers escorted by a cruise director on a major cruise ship. SinglesCruise.com offers a variety of itineraries and types of cruises and will match you with a roommate (same gender, similar age) when possible. Most of its trips are a mix of ages but occasionally it has a sailing for mature singles only, meaning everyone is over the age of 45. Included are private cocktail mixers, theme parties, games, special events, and a separate dining area just for your group where you have opening seating so you may sit with whomever you like.

For information: SinglesCruise.com, 800-393-5000; www .singlescruise.com.

SOLO'S HOLIDAYS

The U.K.'s largest singles tour operator, Solo's Holidays offers hosted group vacations for unattached people. Although it is based in England, it will happily take Americans and Canadians on tour all over the world, giving them a chance to talk, dine, dance, and share experiences with other lone travelers. You'll have a single room with private bath and most holidays have no single supplement. All trips are divided into four groups, for ages 25 to 45, 28 to 55, 39 to 59, and 45-plus, although on many holidays, all ages go together.

For information: Solo's Holidays, 54-58 High St., Edgware, Middlesex HA8 7EJ, England; www.solosholidays.co.uk.

HOOK-UPS FOR SOLO RVers

RVers who travel alone in their motor homes or vans can hook up with others in the same circumstances when they join one of the groups here. All of the clubs provide opportunities to travel together or to meet at campgrounds on the road, making friends with fellow travelers and having a fine time. According to a survey by the Travel Industry Association of America, more than half of RV travelers are 55 or older and retired and tend to take longer-than-average trips.

LONERS ON WHEELS (LOW)

A camping and travel club for mature single men and women, Loners on Wheels is not a lonely hearts club or a matchmaking service but simply an association of friends and extended family who enjoy traveling, camping, RV caravaning, and camaraderie. With 50 chapters located throughout the U.S., Canada, and Mexico, LoW now has a membership of about 2,500 unpartnered travelers. The chapters schedule their own campouts, rallies, and other events during the year at campgrounds, some of which are remote and cost little.

The club's LoW-HI RV Ranch in Deming, New Mexico, offers special rates for club members, two rallies a year,

FOR WOMEN ONLY

Journeywoman.com is a free online resource for women travelers. Packed with female-oriented travel information, tips, advice, and stories designed to inform and inspire solo women of any age to travel safely and happily, it includes a special section for the "50-plus adventuress." Topics range from female-friendly cities around the world to culturally correct clothing, health concerns, safety advice, money-saving tactics, and much more. The site also allows you to sign up for a free quarterly e-newsletter that is full of tips and advice for women who love to travel.

A sister site is HERmail.net, a free e-mail–based service that allows you to connect with other women all over the world who are ready to offer advice and assistance when you visit their cities or countries.

For information: JourneyWoman, 50 Prince Arthur Ave., Toronto, ON M5R 1B5; 416-929-7654; www.journeywoman .com and www.hermail.net.

dances and games in the clubhouse, and occasional forays into Mexico. A monthly newsletter and an annual directory keep everyone up-to-date and in touch.

Annual dues at this writing are $50 U.S. and $56 Canadian, plus a onetime enrollment fee of $5. You'll get an annual directory of members so you can make new friends as you travel and even park in a member's yard.

For information: Loners on Wheels, PO Box 1060-WB, Cape Girardeau, MO 63720; 866-569-2582; www.lonerson wheels.com.

S*M*A*R*T

A club for retired and active members of the U.S. and Canadian armed forces, Special Military Active-Retired Travel Club (S*M*A*R*T) provides social and recreational activities for its more than 3,000 members with "an avid interest in recreational vehicles." Through a network of 60 chapters, it provides seminars and workshops, assists military installations with the improvement of their campgrounds, and sponsors annual rallies.

The club offers several caravans a year in many destinations, including Arkansas, Tennessee, and several western states. It also tours Canada, Mexico, and Alaska, often in fully equipped rented RVs. A national muster, packed with activities, entertainment, seminars, and fellowship, is held every year.

To join, U.S. residents pay an initiation fee of $15 and then $35 a year per family; Canadian residents pay a $20 initiation fee and $40 dues per family, while associate members (disabled, former POWs, Medal of Honor recipients, surviving spouses of eligible members) pay a $15 initiation fee and then $20 a year.

For information: S*M*A*R*T, Inc., 600 University Office Blvd., Pensacola, FL 32504; 800-354-7681 or 850-478-1986; www.smartrving.net.

13

Learning After 50

Have you always wanted to speak Italian, study African birds, examine Eskimo culture, learn to paddle a canoe or ski down a mountain, or delve into archaeology, international finance, the language of whales, or great literature of the 19th century? Now is the time to do it. If you're a typical member of the over-50 generation, you're in good shape, healthy, and alert, with the energy and the time to pursue new interests. So why not go back to school and learn all those things you've always wished you knew? Many of us find it easier and cheaper than ever to go back to school.

Most states have reduced their state university fees for older learners to a mere pittance and, in addition, allow seniors to audit courses for free or close to it. For example, at the University of New Hampshire, state residents who are over 65 may take up to two courses per semester at no cost. At many colleges and universities in Texas, those 65 and over may audit college credit courses with no tuition. If you join California's Over Sixty Program, you'll pay only $3 a semester to earn credit toward a degree. And Cleveland State invites Ohio residents 60 and older to audit up to four courses a semester for free.

Many other colleges offer similar programs. To join the student population at an institution near you, call the admissions office and ask what the deal is for someone your age.

In addition, some special programs as well as entire schools are designed specifically for older students, many of which are affiliated with the Institutes for Learning in Retirement.

A growing number of retirement communities have also formed links with nearby colleges to offer special educational opportunities to their residents. Among them are the Kendel at Ithaca, New York, with ties to Cornell University and Ithaca College, and Oak Hammock, which is affiliated with the University of Florida at Gainesville.

Going back to class is an excellent way to generate feelings of accomplishment and exercise the mind—and one of the best ways to make new friends. It doesn't always mean you'll have to turn in term papers or take excruciatingly difficult exams. Sign up for one class a week on flower arranging or Spanish conversation or a once-a-month lecture series on managing your money. Register as a part-time or full-time student in a traditional university program. Or take a learning vacation on a college campus. Do it *your* way.

You don't even have to attend classes to learn on vacation. You can go on archaeological digs, count butterflies, help save turtles from extinction, brush up on your bassoon playing, listen to opera, search for Roman remains in England, study dancing or Belgian cuisine, or go on safari in Africa.

CHAUTAUQUA INSTITUTION

For more than a century, people have been traveling up to the shores of Lake Chautauqua in southwestern New York, to a cultural summer center set in a quaint Victorian village nestled around a lake. The 856-acre hilltop complex offers a variety of educational programs, including the Residential Week for Older Adults, a Sunday-to-Sunday program every August that includes dormitory lodging, meals, and a gate pass that gets you into all lectures and entertainment for your stay, and to many events at a cost of $650. It fills up far in advance, so if you're interested, don't waste a moment before signing up. In addition, Chautauqua is the host of many Elderhostel programs throughout the year.

For information: Chautauqua Institution, PO Box 28, Chautauqua, NY 14722; 800-836-2787 or 716-357-6250; www.ciweb.org.

THE COLLEGE AT SIXTY

At Fordham University's The College at Sixty where you're welcome at age 50, you can go back to school in a community of peers. Studies begin in small liberal arts seminars taught by Fordham University faculty members in a variety of topics, such as creative writing, art, American presidents, the music of Mozart, and Freudian psychology. You are also entitled to attend an afternoon lecture series and have access to all Fordham facilities. Students who have audited four seminars and decide to matriculate for an undergraduate degree at Fordham College of Liberal Studies are eligible for a 50 percent discount on tuition if they receive Social Security benefits.

For information: The College at Sixty, Fordham College of Liberal Studies, 113 W. 60th St., New York, NY 10023; 212-636-6376; www.fordham.edu/collegeat60.

COLLEGE FOR SENIORS

A membership program for those 50 or older, the College for Seniors is a component of the North Carolina Center for Creative Retirement at the University of North Carolina at Asheville. The courses, most of them taught by peer seniors, range from Chaucer to computers, foreign affairs to opera, and chemistry to tap dancing. The annual fee is currently $40. Added benefits include social events, travel programs, wellness clinics, exploration weekends, library privileges, parking decals, and access to the fitness center.

GOVERNMENT WEBSITE FOR SENIORS

FirstGov for Seniors (www.seniors.gov) is a website specifically for older adults who are seeking information about government services. Maintained by the Social Security Administration, it allows secure and easy access to government sites that provide services and benefits for seniors, references to other sites of special interest to seniors, and links to federal agencies and agencies at the state and local levels in all 50 states. It also provides quick access to helpful services, resources, and information on such subjects as taxes, consumer protection, education, jobs, housing, retirement, health, and travel.

For information: North Carolina Center for Creative Retirement, Reuter Center, CPO #5000, The University of North Carolina at Asheville, One University Hts., Asheville, NC 28804; 828-251-6140; www.unca.edu/ncccr.

ELDERHOSTEL

Elderhostel, with a roster of many thousands of learning vacations, is the world's largest educational travel organization and one of the world's best bargains as well. It is the marketing arm for infinitely varied programs that are provided by a network of educational and cultural sites in all 50 states and about 90 countries. Learning and cultural understanding is a large part of each package, with in-depth lectures, field trips, workshops, and interaction with local experts woven into each day. The only requirement for participation is that you are 55 or older (an accompanying adult companion may be younger). You need no previous educational background, just intense interest in your destination and the designated subject. The programs offer classes on every conceivable topic taught by the host institution's faculty, staff, and local experts and include excursions and social activities. Identify your interest and you'll undoubtedly find a matching program, from archaeology to Shakespeare to biking to Ireland or Thailand or culinary arts.

Most of the programs in the U.S. are five- or six-nighters, although there are also one-day and weekend excursions to major American cities. Those in foreign countries last for one to four weeks and include transportation. The many offerings are listed in voluminous seasonal catalogs and also on Elderhostel's website where you may search by subject, date, or location. And they come in many categories.

ELDERHOSTEL SCHOLARSHIPS

Elderhostel offers a limited number of full or partial scholarships, to be used only in the U.S. and Canada, for people who find the tuition costs of the programs beyond their means. Funds to cover travel costs are not included, and eligibility is determined upon completion of an application that includes a confidential questionnaire. Scholarship programs in Alaska and Hawaii are available only to residents of those states.

For information: Elderhostel, 11 Avenue de Lafayette, Boston, MA 02111. Attention: Scholarships.

For example, the Adventures Afloat programs use ships, boats, and barges as a way to visit and study remote places. Discover North America features on-the-move itineraries, listed by geographic region and theme. Active Outdoor packages include activities such as canoeing, skiing, biking, and walking (see Chapter 14). Escorted tours take you all over the world. Train Treks uses trains as moving classrooms, combining rail travel with learning.

Intergenerational and family programs for members and their children or grandchildren are another option, as is Road Scholars for adults of all ages that takes small groups for behind-the-scenes experiences in little-known places.

And, finally, Service Learning programs connect you to volunteer organizations that need your help (see Chapter 19).

For information: Elderhostel, 11 Avenue de Lafayette, Boston, MA 02111; 877-426-8056 or 617-426-7788; www .elderhostel.org.

NATIONAL ACADEMY OF OLDER CANADIANS (NAOC)

Based in Vancouver, the NAOC's mission is to involve Canadians over the age of 45 in lifelong learning and to help them keep pace with modern technology. It offers computer classes with "senior-friendly" courses. The membership fee is $17 (Canadian) a year.

For information: National Academy of Older Canadians, 411 Dunsmuir St., Vancouver, BC V6B 1X4; 604-681-3767; www.vcn.bc.ca/naoc.

OASIS

OASIS is a nonprofit organization sponsored by the May Department Stores Company in collaboration with local hospitals, medical centers, government agencies, and other participants through a network of centers in 26 cities across the nation. Its purpose is to enrich the lives of people over 50 by providing programs in the arts, humanities, wellness, technology, and volunteer service to its members. At its centers, OASIS offers classes ranging from French conversation and the visual arts to dance, bridge, creative writing, history, exercise, classical music, points of law, and prevention of osteoporosis. There are also special events such as concerts, plays, museum visits, lectures, and even trips and cruises. Membership is free.

For information: The OASIS Institute, 7710 Carondelet Ave., St. Louis, MO 63105; 314-862-2933; www.oasisnet.org.

SEMESTER AT SEA

A 100-day educational voyage around the world, Semester at Sea, academically sponsored by the University of Virginia and administered by the Institute for Shipboard Education, takes more than 600 college students and about 60 "senior scholars" on a unique learning experience that is designed to advance the exchange of understanding and knowledge among cultures. The *M. V. Explorer*, a former passenger ship refitted as a floating campus, circumnavigates the Earth twice a year, visiting countries that have included Japan, China, India, Malaysia, Kenya, Brazil, Venezuela, Egypt, Israel, South Africa, Greece, Turkey, Vietnam, and Morocco.

While the college students earn credit hours toward an undergraduate degree, the older participants may audit classes or enroll for full credit, choosing from among 60 courses taught by faculty from various universities. Onboard courses range from anthropology and biological sciences to economics, fine arts, philosophy, political science, and religion. Lengthy stays in each port of call give students a chance to experience the peoples and cultures firsthand.

Amenities include an adult coordinator, entertainment, buffet-style meals, lectures, discussion groups, guest scholars with expertise in local cultures, films, art shows, sports, and more.

In addition to the long voyages scheduled during the spring and fall, a new, condensed 65-day summertime Semester at Sea combines a smaller number of college students and seniors. From Vancouver, B.C., to Sitka, Alaska, then to Vladavlostok, Pusan, Shanghai, Hanoi, Keelung, and Osaka to Seattle, the group travels aboard the *M.V. Explorer*, learning all the way.

For information: Institute for Shipboard Education, PO Box 400885, Charlottesville, VA 22904; 800-854-0195; www.semesteratsea.com.

SENIOR SUMMER SCHOOL

You can go back to the college life again, choosing among six different university campuses around the country. Senior Summer School offers two- to six-week educational vacations in the summer, as well as three days to a week in the fall and winter, all taught by university instructors and local professionals. Courses are college level, but there are no grades, compulsory papers, mandatory attendance, or previous educational requirements.

In the summer program, accommodations and cafeteria meals are in dormitories, hotels, residence hall suites, and private apartments. Students are a mix of couples and singles, and you may choose to take whatever classes you like in a range of subjects. Sightseeing trips, excursions, weekly housekeeping, and social activities are all part of the deal.

In 2008, locations include: Albuquerque, New Mexico; Appalachian State University at Boone, North Carolina; St. Michael's College in Burlington, Vermont; Colorado College at Colorado Springs; University of Wisconsin at Madison; West Virginia University at Morgantown; University of Hawaii at Hilo; Philadelphia; and San Diego State at San Diego.

For information: Senior Summer School, 4400 W. Sample Rd., Coconut Creek, FL 33442; 800-847-2466 or 954-917-9690; www.seniorsummerschool.com.

SENIOR VENTURES IN OREGON

Sign up at Southern Oregon University in Ashland for one- or two-week educational theater programs exclusively for people at least 50 years of age (and companions who may be younger). The summer programs coincide with Ashland's famous annual Oregon Shakespeare Festival, and classes are taught by actors, backstage professionals, and Shakespearean scholars. You stay on campus and eat your meals there. Added bonus: theater tickets to current productions. A few travel adventures, such as a Canadian theater expedition, are also offered.

For information: Senior Ventures, Southern Oregon University, 1250 Siskiyu Blvd., Ashland, OR 97520; 800-257-0577 or 541-552-7672; www.sou.edu/seniorventures.

UTAH STATE UNIVERSITY SUMMER CITIZENS

Spend May to August at Utah State University in Logan where about 1,000 seniors participate in the Summer Citizens Program and choose from a variety of courses taught by university professors and local experts, attend cultural events, live in student housing, participate in recreational activities, and enjoy the pleasant temperatures.

An ID card that costs $70 is your ticket to the program and gets you into all parts of the campus from theaters to libraries, computer labs, exercise rooms, tennis courts,

SENIORNET

SeniorNet has taught thousands of 50+ adults to use computers. A nonprofit organization, it sponsors about 250 SeniorNet Learning Centers in diverse settings from shopping centers to churches around the country, staffed by volunteers, where members can learn to understand and use computers. Independent members participate through the organization's electronic community, SeniorNet Online.

To take the classes at a learning center, you must join SeniorNet for $40 a year ($60 for two years), which gives you other benefits too, including a quarterly newsletter; discounts on computer-related books, software, and hardware; and invitations to conferences and meetings.

It costs nothing to access SeniorNet Online, where you may join any of hundreds of discussion groups and share information and opinions about myriad subjects from computers to politics, the arts, and health.

A new SeniorNet program, Retired Technology Volunteers (RTV), trains and supports volunteers over 50 who help community and nonprofit organizations to expand their technological capabilities.

For information: SeniorNet, 900 Lafayette St., Santa Clara, CA 95050; 800-747-6848 or 408-615-0699; www.senior net.org.

parking lots, and the swimming pool. Your inexpensive housing may be on campus or off, and free shuttles and buses take you everywhere you want to go at the university or in the city.

Three-week packages are also available for those with less time to spend getting smart.

For information: Summer Citizens Program, Utah State University, 5005 Old Main Hill, Logan, UT 84322; 800-538-2663 or 435-797-7573; www.summercitizens.usu.edu.

LIFELONG LEARNING INSTITUTES (LLI)

Another way to learn with a group of contemporaries is to join an LLI, a community-based organization of retirement-age students in hundreds of communities in the U.S. Most of these institutes are member-run under the auspices of a host college or university. Each is independent and unique, providing noncredit academic programs developed and often led by the members themselves. The institutes have an open membership for retirement-age students regardless of previous education and charge modest membership fees. There are no exams, degrees, papers, or homework.

Many of these learning centers are members of a voluntary association, the Elderhostel Institute Network, that provides information and encourages the development of new programs in more local communities. Others are funded by the Osher Foundation that now operates a network of 119 Osher Lifelong Learning Institutes throughout the U.S. and gives awards to other already-established LLI schools. Its National Resource Center facilitates the exchange of information among schools.

For information: Elderhostel Institute Network, 11 Avenue de Lafayette, Boston, MA 02111; 877-426-8056 or 617-426-7788; www.elderhostel.org. National Resource Center, Osher Foundation, PO Box 9300, Portland, ME 04104; 207-780-4128; www.osher.net.

14

Good Deals for
Good Sports

Real sports never give up their sneakers. If you've been a physically active person all your life, you're certainly not going to turn into a couch potato now—especially since you've probably got more time, energy, and maybe funds than you ever had before to enjoy athletic activities. Besides, you can now take advantage of some interesting special privileges and adventures offered exclusively to people over the age of 49.

ELDERHOSTEL

Many Elderhostel programs (see Chapter 13) include a wide selection of outdoor and sports activities for beginners as well as experienced athletes. Among the choices are golf, birding, walking and trekking, tennis, hiking, biking, sea kayaking, sailing, whitewater rafting, wilderness canoeing, skiing, snowshoeing, and trail biking.

For information: Elderhostel, 11 Avenue de Lafayette, Boston, MA 02111; 877-426-8056 or 617-426-7788; www .elderhostel.org.

EXPLORATIONS IN TRAVEL

Exclusively for women over the age of 40, Explorations in Travel's action-filled itineraries are geared for energetic grown-up women who love the outdoors and prefer to travel with contemporaries, leaving the men behind. Typical trips include hiking and rafting in Oregon; canoeing the Rio Grande; cruising the Erie Canal; exploring New Zealand; or lodge-based hiking in Norway. An occasional intergenerational trip is planned for mothers and daughters and other female relative and friend combinations with one participant required to be 40, the other at least 21. Several weekend adventures are also usually scheduled.

For information: Explorations in Travel, 2458 River Rd., Guilford, VT 05301; 877-257-0152 or 802-257-0152; www .exploretravel.com.

OUTWARD BOUND WILDERNESS

Outward Bound is famous for its rugged wilderness survival trips for young people with the purpose of building self-confidence, self-esteem, and the ability to work as a team. But it also offers short adventure courses specifically for adults over the age of 30, with many participants well over 50. Among recent courses for these mature adventurers: backpacking in the Blue Ridge Mountains and canoeing in the Boundary Waters of Minnesota.

For information: Outward Bound Wilderness, 910 Jackson St., Golden, CO 80401; 866-467-7640; www.outwardbound wilderness.org.

OVER THE HILL GANG (OTHG)

This is a club that welcomes fun-loving, adventurous people from 50 to 90-plus (and younger spouses or companions) who are looking for action and contemporaries to pursue it with. No naps, no rockers, no sitting by the pool sipping margaritas. OTHG started as a ski club many years ago (see Chapter 15), but its members can now be found participating in all kinds of activities when the ski season ends. Recent trips have included fully escorted trips to ski areas in the West, Europe, and South America. Other options offered include whitewater rafting in Oregon, sailing and biking in Croatia, biking from Hanoi to Saigon, hiking in Slovakia and Poland, and golfing in Whistler, B.C.

The club currently has about 6,000 members in 50 states and 14 countries. The annual membership fee ($60 single, $80 for a couple) brings you a quarterly magazine, discounts, information about national and chapter events, and a chance to join the fun.

For information: Over the Hill Gang International, 1515 N. Tejon St., Dept. G, Colorado Springs, CO 80907; 719-389-0022; www.othgi.com.

BIKE TRIPS FOR 50-PLUS

Biking has become one of America's most popular sports, and people who never dreamed they could go much farther than around the block are now pedaling up to 50 miles in a day. That includes over-the-hill bikers as well as young-sters of 16, 39, or 49. In fact, some tours and clubs are designated specifically for over-50s.

COMPASS HOLIDAYS

For a cycling break in the heart of England—the Cotswolds, Bath and Wiltshire, Cornwall, the Severn Vail, and the Lake District—look into the guided or self-planned biking tours from Compass Holidays. With a guide, you can ride for three days, for example, around Bourton-on-the-Water, or seven days in the Cotswolds, starting and ending in Cheltenham. You can also ride on your own with maps, planned accommodations, and luggage transfers on circular routes along quiet country roads from village to village near Bath or Malmesbury. Your luggage is transported for you. For bikers over 50, Compass Holidays—which also schedules walking tours—offers a 10 percent discount if you take a seven-night tour and 5 percent when you book tours of two nights or more and mention this book. Take your own bike or rent one there.

For this company's excursions on foot, see Walking and Hiking later in this chapter.

For information: Compass Holidays, Cheltenham Spa Railway Station, Queens Rd., Cheltenham, Gloucestershire GL51 8NP, UK; www.compass-holidays.com.

CROSS CANADA CYCLE TOUR SOCIETY

This is a bicycling club for retired people who love to jump on their bikes and take off across the countryside. Most of the club's members are over 60, with many in their 70s and

80s and only a few under 50. Says the society, "Our aim is to stay alive as long as possible." Now there's a worthwhile goal.

Based in British Columbia, with members—both men and women, skilled and novice—mostly in British Columbia, Ontario, and Alberta, but many in the U.S., this club organizes many trips a year, all led by volunteer tour guides. Membership costs $30 single or $45 per couple per year and includes a monthly newsletter to keep you up-to-date on happenings.

Several times a week local members gather for day rides, and a few times a year there are longer club trips to such far-ranging locations as Cuba, Hawaii, New Zealand, the Netherlands, and U.S. national parks. Every few years a group of intrepid bikers pedals clear across Canada, an adventure that takes a few weeks to accomplish, with some members dropping in and out along the way. Many of the longer trips are tenting or camping tours, while others put you up in hostels, motels, or hotels.

For information: Cross Canada Cycle Tour Society, 186-8120 No. 2 Rd., Richmond, BC V7C 5J8; 604-313-0850; www.cccts.org.

ELDERHOSTEL BICYCLE TOURS

Elderhostel's famous educational travel programs include both domestic and foreign bicycle tours among its many offerings. These vary by the season and year and are all listed in the organization's frequent and voluminous catalogs. Recent programs in the U.S. have included six-day inn-to-inn pedals along the Erie Canal in New York, the northwest corner of Arizona, and the rolling hills of Texas. Lectures and sightseeing excursions are included.

Bike tours in foreign lands are scheduled from April through September in Canada, Denmark, England, Italy, Germany, Austria, France, and the Netherlands. Led by a guide and riding as a group, you cover 25 to 35 miles a day and learn about the culture and history from local educators and other specialists. Three-speed bikes are provided, as are breakfast, dinner, and accommodations in small hotels. The support van that travels with the group to carry the luggage and repair equipment will carry you as well if you decide that you can't possibly make it up another hill.

For information: Elderhostel, 11 Avenue de Lafayette, Boston, MA 02111; 877-426-8056 or 617-426-7788; www .elderhostel.org.

50PLUS EXPEDITIONS

Take a bike trip with this company and you'll have plenty of time to see the sights and stop at the nearest castle along the way because its tours are planned for your age group. You must be an active sort, however, who has pedaled many a mile before. Most of the trips are self-guided with accommodations and two meals a day included. There's a van to carry your luggage and you, if necessary; comfortable bikes and up to 12 companions. Upcoming tours, usually eight days long, are in Ireland's Dingle Peninsula, along the Danube in Austria, and from Vienna to Budapest.

For information: 50plus Expeditions, 760 Lawrence Ave. West, Toronto, ON M6A 3E7; 866-318-5050 or 416-749-5150; www.50plusexpeditions.com.

INTERNATIONAL BICYCLE TOURS (IBT)

The Fifty Plus Tours by IBT are planned for bikers over 50 who are not interested in pedaling up mountains but love to hit the road on two wheels. They go to Sicily, Cape Cod, Sweden, Germany, and England, among other places, on leisurely eight-day rides along bicycle paths and quiet country roads on flat terrain through farmland, forests, islands, and small villages. You cover only about 30 miles a day, so there's plenty of time for sightseeing, snacking, shopping, and relaxing. You lodge in small hotels and dine on local specialties.

Among IBT's other adventures are 14-day bike-and-barge tours in the Netherlands where you sleep and eat aboard 22-passenger, 147-foot barges that motor along the sea and through the canals and rivers of rural Holland and bike during the daylight hours to see the sights up close.

For information: International Bicycle Tours, PO Box 754, Essex, CT 06426; 860-767-7005; www.internationalbicycle tours.com.

OVER THE HILL GANG (OTHG)

OTHG, a club for energetic 50-plus adventurers whose main activity is skiing, schedules at least a couple of group bike tours every year, usually in Europe along routes rated "easy" on gentle terrain. Bike during the day; sleep at small hotels along the way at night. See more information about the club and its activities earlier in this chapter.

For information: Over the Hill Gang International, 1515 N. Tejon St., Dept. G, Colorado Springs, CO 80907; 719-389-0022; www.othgi.com.

VBT BICYCLING VACATIONS

This venerable bike company, now an affiliate of Grand Circle Travel, an agency that specializes in travel for people over the age of 50, has tailored many of its trips for the same fast-growing age group. Although challenging routes remain for those who want them, many of the itineraries in the U.S. and overseas are less demanding and their schedules more relaxed. VBT's biking vacations currently include a number of Easy Tours eminently suitable for older bikers who seek adventure without all that much physical stress, such as a tour of Tuscany riding along the coast on less-traveled roads.

For information: VBT, 614 Monkton Rd., Bristol, VT 05443; 800-245-3868 or 802-453-4811; www.vbt.com.

WOMANTOURS

Bicycle trips for women are the specialty of this group that schedules many tours suitable for older bikers with moderate terrain and easy mileage. Recent trips have gone to the Finger Lakes, wine country, Blue Ridge Mountains, Glacier National Park, and Hawaii's Big Island. A van goes along with every group to carry the luggage, repair equipment, and give weary riders a lift. There's also a much more ambitious 58-day, 4,250-mile trip scheduled every year exclusively for women over 50. You'll paddle all the way through rural America from San Diego, California, to St. Augustine, Florida. Mileage averages 57 miles a day, mostly on fairly flat terrain, with one rest day per week. For this trip you'd better be in good shape!

For information: WomanTours, 2340 Elmwood Ave., Rochester, NY 14618; 800-247-1444; www.womantours.com.

TENNIS, ANYONE?

An estimated three million of the nation's tennis players are over 50, with the number increasing every year as more of

SENIOR CYCLING

Exclusively for bikers over 50 who prefer to travel with congenial contemporaries, the bicycle adventures by Senior Cycling (a.k.a. Old Folks on Spokes) may do the job. You'll do the miles but at slower speeds than 20-somethings, taking time to enjoy the journey and make stops along the way. When overnights are required, you'll stay at hotels or B&Bs and dine at local eateries. Trips range from one- or two-day ventures out of the Washington, D.C., area to a seven-day spin along the Erie Canal. Other choices, for two to six days, include the Florida Keys, the Katy Trail in Missouri, Pennsylvania's Amish country, and the towpaths of the C & O Canal in Maryland. Plus trips to Tuscany, the Loire Valley, and Sicily.

Tours are rated for difficulty, with several featuring flat, easy terrain for rank beginners. Groups are small, from 6 to 12 participants, plus a guide and a support vehicle to carry luggage, lunch, and you, if necessary. Accommodations and most meals are included. Bring your own bike or rent one. *For information:* Senior Cycling, 37419 Branch River Rd., Loudon Heights, VA 20132; 540-668-6307; www.senior cycling.com.

us decide to forgo playing canasta for a few fast sets on the courts. You need only a court, a racket, a can of balls, and an opponent to play tennis, but if you'd like to be competitive or sociable, you may want to get into some senior tournaments.

UNITED STATES TENNIS ASSOCIATION (USTA)

The USTA offers a wide variety of tournaments for players over the advanced age of 35, at both local and national levels. To participate, you must be a member ($60 per year). When you join, you will become a member of a regional section, receive periodic schedules of USTA-sponsored tournaments and events in your area for which you can sign up, get a discount on tennis books and publications, and receive a monthly magazine and a free subscription to *Tennis* magazine.

In the schedule of tournaments, you'll find competitions listed for specific five-year age groups: for men from 35 to 90-plus and for women from 35 to 85-plus. In addition, self-rated tournaments match you up with people of all ages who play at your level. If you feel you're good enough to compete, send for an application and sign up. There is usually a modest fee.

For information: USTA, 70 W. Red Oak Ln., West Harrison, NY 10604; 800-990-8782 or 914-696-7000; www.usta .com.

USTA LEAGUE TENNIS, SENIOR DIVISION

If you want to compete with other 50-plus tennis players in local, area, and sectional competitions culminating in a national championship, join the Senior Division of the USTA League Tennis program. Your level of play will be rated in a specific skill category ranging from beginner to advanced, and you'll compete only with people on your own ability level. You must join USTA ($60 a year) for the privilege and the details.

For information: USTA, 70 W. Red Oak Ln., West Harrison, NY 10604; 800-990-8782 or 914-696-7000; www.usta .com.

VAN DER MEER TENNIS UNIVERSITY

Van der Meer Tennis University offers five-day Seniors Clinics from September to May every year at its Van der Meer Shipyard Tennis Resort on Hilton Head Island. Specifically for 50-plus players, beginning or experienced, the clinics provide more than 16 hours of instruction, including video analysis, tactics and strategies for singles and doubles, and match play drills, plus social activities and free court time. The goal is to improve your strokes and game strategy so you'll get more enjoyment out of your game. Discounted accommodations are available for participants.

For information: Van der Meer Tennis University, PO Box 5902, Hilton Head Island, SC 29938; 800-845-6138 or 843-785-8388; www.vdmtennis.com.

WALKING AND HIKING

Walking tours have become remarkably popular among people of all ages but especially ours. We're old enough to appreciate the close encounters with the world that moving along on our own two feet allows. Some tour companies specialize in tours specifically for mature participants.

APPALACHIAN MOUNTAIN CLUB (AMC)

Every year this famous hiking club, the oldest conservation and recreation organization in the U.S., schedules a few inexpensive two- to five-day Elderhostel treks for people over the age of 55. You'll hike two to eight miles a day at an easy pace in New Hampshire's White Mountains or the

Catskills in New York and sleep in a comfortable lodge at night, with plenty of time to savor the scenery and glimpse the wildlife. Routes vary from year to year. Yearly membership fee in AMC for adults is $50 ($75 per family), but if you are 69 or over, you pay only $25.

For information: Appalachian Mountain Club, 5 Joy St., Boston, MA 02108; 617-523-0655; www.outdoors.org. Elderhostel, 877-626-8056.

COMPASS HOLIDAYS

This company specializes in walking and cycling holidays in the English countryside, with or without a guide. You'll enjoy walks through quiet villages, bustling towns, and pastoral countrysides for three to eight days, covering only a few miles, stopping each evening at a small family hotel for local food and a comfortable night's sleep. If you are over the age of 50 and you sign up for a seven-night break, you'll get a 10 percent discount if you mention this book. Compass also offers many bike tours in England.

For information: Compass Holidays, Cheltenham Spa Railway Station, Queens Rd., Cheltenham, Gloucestershire GL51 8NP, UK; www.compass-holidays.com.

ELDERHOSTEL WALKING AND HIKING PROGRAMS

Both Elderhostel's domestic and international programs include walking and hiking tours for practiced walkers with energy and good health. Accompanied by guides, lecturers, and local specialists, the overseas walkers, carrying small day packs, cover 4 to 12 miles a day, rain or shine. You'll stay and dine mostly in small hotels, while lunch is taken en route. Educational programs are part of the package. Trekking trips are also on Elderhostel's menu, taking you up to eight miles a day on footpaths in Nepal or Switzerland. For these you must be in even better physical shape and accustomed to vigorous exercise.

For information: Elderhostel, 11 Avenue de Lafayette, Boston, MA 02111; 877-426-8056 or 617-426-7788; www .elderhostel.org.

ELDERTREKS

On these trekking trips in the Far East, all of them for 50-plus travelers accompanied by guides, cooks, and porters, you hike overland on foot and sleep in small inns, a village house, or maybe a tent. The trips are rated for difficulty so you may choose one that matches your abilities. For more information, see Chapter 9.

For information: ElderTreks, 597 Markham St., Toronto, ON M6G 2L7; 800-741-7956 or 416-588-5000; www.elder treks.com.

50PLUS EXPEDITIONS

This company plans its adventures exclusively for people of a certain age—50 or more—so don't expect its hiking trips to be so strenuous that you won't be able to keep up with the pack. Sure, you'll hike all day, but you choose whether you want easy, moderate, or difficult terrain. And you can always climb aboard the accompanying van if you can't take another step. You will have comfortable accommodations and eat tasty local meals as you trek through such scenic places as the Alps in Austria, the Cotswolds in England, Ireland's Dingle Peninsula, or the path from Vienna to Prague.

For information: 50plus Expeditions, 760 Lawrence Ave. West, Toronto, ON M6A 3E7; 866-318-5050 or 416-749-5150; www.50plusexpeditions.com.

RIVER ODYSSEYS WEST (ROW)

If you love wilderness rivers but aren't into whitewater rafting (see Chapter 9), consider ROW's raft-supported walking tours along trails that follow the course of the Middle Fork of the Salmon River in Idaho or the Snake River in Hells Canyon on the Oregon border. These tours are created specifically for Boomers and seniors ages 50 to 85 in good condition. Carrying only a day pack and led by a guide, you hike six or eight miles a day with plenty of time to smell the flowers and spot the wildlife. A cargo raft carries all the camping gear and your luggage as well as the food and other supplies, and a smaller support raft floats along at the group's pace to act as a sag wagon for tired walkers. When you arrive at camp each afternoon, the staff has already set up the roomy tents and the kitchen and has started cooking dinner, giving you time to relax, fish, or explore.

For information: River Odysseys West, PO Box 579-UD, Coeur d'Alene, ID 83816; 800-451-6034 or 208-765-0841; www.rowadventures.com.

SIERRA CLUB

Several hiking and backpacking trips planned for 50-plus participants are among the Sierra Club's list of outings every summer. Led by volunteers, you'll hike in such places as the Shenandoah National Park and Tahoe National Forest. Backpack adventures have included trips to the Weminuche Wilderness in Colorado and the Wind River Range in Wyoming. You must belong to the club to participate, but if you are a senior, your yearly membership costs only $25 instead of the usual adult fee of $39.

For information: Sierra Club Outings, 85 Second St., San Francisco, CA 94105; 415-977-5500; www.sierraclub.org/outings/national.

WALK YOUR WAY

Many of Walk Your Way Into the Heart of England trips are designed for older walkers. These are 12- to 15-day accompanied tours off the beaten path in such quaint and picturesque areas as the Channel Islands, the Cotswolds, and the Isle of Man. Some walks are circular, beginning and ending in the same village, averaging five miles a day. Others are linear, covering eight to ten miles a day. The group is never larger than ten, lodging is in family guest houses or bed-and-breakfasts, and evening meals are eaten in local pubs.

For information: Walk Your Way, PO Box 231, Red Feather Lakes, CO 80545; 970-881-2709; www.walkyourway.co.uk.

WALKING THE WORLD

Anyone over 50 who loves adventure and is in good physical shape is invited to participate in Walking the World's explorations. These are 7- to 11-day backcountry treks, covering six to ten miles a day, that focus on natural and cultural history. On some trips, you'll camp out and, carrying only a day pack, hike to each new destination. On others, you will lodge in small country inns, hotels, or bed-and-breakfasts, setting forth on daily walks into the countryside. Groups are small, from 12 to 18 participants plus two local guides, and there's no upper age limit. No previous hiking experience is necessary.

Destinations have included Bryce and Zion National Parks in Utah; Banff and Jasper National Parks in the Canadian Rockies; and Costa Rica, as well as Europe and Hawaii.

For information: Walking the World, PO Box 1186, Fort Collins, CO 80522; 866-393-9255 or 970-498-0500; www .walkingtheworld.com.

ADVENTURES IN THE SNOW
SENIOR WORLD TOURS

Explore the winter wonders of Yellowstone National Park or the Snowy Range in Wyoming aboard your own quiet, four-stroke snowmobile on a seniors-only, seven-day adventure trip, limited to 16 participants age 50 or over. All tours travel on roadways already groomed for the use of park personnel—and never off-road, where snowmobiles can damage the environment. Included in the package are driving lessons, snowmobiles, fuel, boots, gloves, helmets, cross-country skis, meals, and trusty guides. No experience is necessary, but don't even think of going unless you enjoy the snow and are in decent physical condition.

By the way, if you go with a companion who does not care to ride alone, you may choose a two-up machine that allows the two of you to travel tandem. Nonriders can go by snow coach.

On the Yellowstone National Park trip, you'll ride your snowmobile through the park to view the wildlife, geysers, hot springs, mountain passes, awesome views, and splendid scenery, overnighting in wilderness lodges and resorts. If you choose to ride in the Snowy Range of Wyoming, your tour takes you to Medicine Bow Routt National Forest near Laramie. Choose the Montana itinerary and you'll go to a lodge in Whitefish to ride, ski, dogsled, ice-skate, or kick back.

For information: Senior World Tours, 2205 N. River Rd., Fremont, OH 43420; 888-355-1686 or 419-355-1686; www.seniorworldtours.com.

APPALACHIAN MOUNTAIN CLUB (AMC)

Famous for its hiking programs in New England, AMC also schedules several affordable cross-country skiing and snow-shoeing courses for grown-ups every winter. The 50+ Cross Country Skiing for Beginners program gives you a chance to join a small group of peers for two nights at an inn in the Catskills or the White Mountains where you'll get accommodations, meals, and lessons on groomed trails. The 50+ Snowshoe Adventure is a similar program for beginners who want to learn the basics about navigating on top of the snow. To participate, you need to be in good physical condition and able to carry a full day pack. Members of the club are entitled to a 10 percent discount on the cost of these adventures. The annual adult membership fee for AMC is $50 ($75 for a family) but only $25 for those 69 or over.

For information: Appalachian Mountain Club, 5 Joy St., Boston, MA 02108; 617-523-0655; www.outdoors.org.

MOTORCYCLE HEAVEN
BEACH'S MOTORCYCLE ADVENTURES

If motorcycling is your passion and adventure is in your blood, look into the motorcycle tours offered by the Beach family who has been conducting cycling tours since 1972. All ages, including yours, may choose from a variety of trips in the Alps, New Zealand, Italy, and California. You must, of course, have a valid motorcycle license. Motorcycles are provided in your choice of available models and there is no mileage charge. A guide goes along with you, and your luggage is carried by a van. By the way, both bikes and automobiles are welcome on these tours, so if friends or family want to join you they may go along in a car.

You're on your own during the day, following a tour book that gives daily itineraries, road maps, distances, estimated en route times, business hours, sightseeing ideas, good (and bad) roads, suggestions for activities, driving tips, and directions to the hotel of the night. The daily routing, pace, and stops are up to you. There are several riding options each day, so you may decide to cruise along or ride long and hard. Every evening, you'll meet the group and your guide at a hotel or family farm where you'll eat dinner that night and have breakfast the next morning.

For information: Beach's Motorcycle Adventures, 2763 W. River Pky., Grand Island, NY 14072; 716-773-4960; www.bmca.com.

RETREADS MOTORCYCLE CLUB

Members of Retreads, an association of motorcycle enthusiasts, all 40-plus with an average age of 60 and a few in their

80s, get together for state, regional, and international rallies to talk cycling and ride together. Each state association and local chapter (there are more than 40 in Florida) also has regular get-togethers for short jaunts and socializing. Started as a correspondence club in 1969, Retreads has grown to more than 5,000 members—men and women—in the U.S., Canada, the U.K., and New Zealand. Annual contribution is $15 a year per person or $20 per couple. A club newsletter keeps members informed of the activities.

For information: Retreads Motorcycle Club International, 528 N. Main St., Albany, IN 47320; 765-789-4070; www .retreads.org.

GOLF VACATIONS

Most municipal and many private golf courses offer senior golfers (usually at 60 or 65) a discount off the regular greens fees, at least on certain days of the week. Take along identification and ask for your discount when you reserve a tee time. You can often find discounts too on golf carts, lessons, and driving ranges.

THE GOLF CARD

Designed especially for senior golfers, the Golf Card entitles members to free greens fees at about 1,000 participating golf courses in the U.S., Canada, and the Caribbean, and up to 50 percent off the combined cart and greens fee for two rounds a year at an additional 2,400 courses, plus stay-and-play packages at more than 200 resorts. Members, who pay $49 for the first year and $65 thereafter, also receive an annual *Golf Traveler Directory* and quarterly newsletters that keep them up-to-date.

For information: The Golf Card, PO Box 7021, Englewood, CO 80155; 800-321-8269 or 303-790-2267; www.golfcard .com.

JOHN JACOBS GOLF SCHOOLS

Golfers over the age of 62 get a discount of 10 percent on the cost of golf packages offered July through December at any John Jacobs Golf School. You'll learn how to improve your game while you play at some of the finest courses in the country. Most packages include lodging, meals, instruction, course time, greens fees, and cart. Commuter packages are available with a senior discount at all 45 schools.

For information: John Jacobs Golf Schools, 6210 McKellips Rd., Mesa, AZ 85215; 800-472-5007 or 480-991-8587; www.jacobsgolf.com.

OVER THE HILL GANG (OTHG)

In the off-season when there's little or no snow for its members to ski on, this club for peppy people over the age of 50 always plans at least one group golf vacation every year at a well-known golf resort. See more information about the club and its activities earlier in this chapter.

For information: Over the Hill Gang International, 1515 N. Tejon St., Dept. G, Colorado Springs, CO 80907; 719-389-0022; www.othgi.com.

SENIOR GOLFERS ASSOCIATION OF AMERICA (SGA)

An association of amateur senior and super-senior golfers, SGA invites its members, all of them 50 or older, to travel to some of the best golf resorts in the country, stay in deluxe accommodations, and compete in friendly tournaments. Vacations include four nights' lodging and dinner reservations, three or four days of golf, plus banquets, award ceremonies, dances, cocktail parties, tours, shopping sprees, special events for nongolfing spouses, you name it. SGA handles all the details, but you must provide your own transportation to the resort. Tournaments scheduled every month at top-notch resorts are based on your handicap and your age. Membership costs $50 a year.

Among the requirements for membership are that you are well-mannered and well-groomed on and off the golf course, can play a round in less than 4-1/2 hours, will play the game according to the rules with integrity and etiquette, are pleasant to be with—even when things are not going right—and are at least 50 years of age.

For information: Senior Golfers Association of America, 3013 Church St., Myrtle Beach, SC 29577; 800-337-0047 or 843-626-8100; www.seniorgolfersamerica.com.

WATER AEROBICS
FUN & FITNESS TRAVEL CLUB

The aerobic vacations scheduled once a month by the Fun & Fitness Travel Club, a club for mature adults, feature water exercise classes every morning on every one of its cruises to places like the Caribbean, Alaska, the East Coast, and the Mexican Riviera, supplemented by other forms of daily physical activities, including yoga, tai chi, deck walking, ballroom dancing, and chair aerobics. The club—no dues required—is especially popular among single seniors.

For information: Fun & Fitness Club, 7338 Dartford Dr., Ste. 9, McLean, VA 22102; 800-955-9942 or 703-827-0414; www.fun-fitness.com.

FITNESS
LIFELONG FITNESS ALLIANCE

Formed by a group of exercise researchers at Stanford University almost 30 years ago, this organization's mission is to promote fitness and an active lifestyle for people over the age of 50. It sponsors active programs, including an annual Dare to Be Fit Weekend and a Fitness Challenge Camp every July on the Stanford campus, and it publishes a quarterly newsletter. Its members from almost every state serve as volunteers for ongoing studies on "active aging" and act as ambassadors to help promote and lead fitness activities in their own communities.

For information: Lifelong Fitness Alliance, 658 Bair Island Rd., Redwood City, CA 94063; 650-361-8282; www.50plus .org.

OVER-50 SOFTBALL
INTERNATIONAL SENIOR SOFTBALL ASSOCIATION (ISSA)

ISSA, an association that was founded to promote softball for men and women over the age of 50, conducts the World Championship Tournaments every year in Virginia for more than 300 senior teams. Players who are members of senior leagues and local softball associations all over the U.S. may join and so may individuals without affiliation. Members receive a master nationwide tournament schedule, the results of all national tournaments, and the rankings of all senior softball teams.

For information: ISSA, 9401 East St., Manassas, VA 20110; 703-368-1188; www.seniorsoftball.org.

NATIONAL ASSOCIATION OF SENIOR CIRCUIT SOFTBALL (NASCS)

The NASCS is an organization composed of several thousand softball players and hundreds of teams, with a goal of encouraging senior softball programs in the U.S. and Canada. To play ball on one of its teams, you must be at least 50 years old and pay an annual $35 fee ($10 if you are over 80). There's no upper age limit, with players up to age 85. Both men and women are welcomed. NASCS runs qualifying tournaments for the annual Senior Softball World Series, when more than 125 teams from the U.S. and Canada compete in a major ballpark. A semiannual magazine, *Line Drive*, keeps members up-to-date on happenings here and abroad.

For information: NASCS, PO Box 1085, Mt. Clemens, MI 48046; 517-393-0505; www.nascs.org.

SENIOR SOFTBALL–USA

This organization, the largest senior softball group in the world, conducts softball tournaments all over the country and organizes international tournaments as well, including the Senior Softball World Championship Games held in September. Anyone over 50, man or woman, in the U.S. and Canada may join for a $15 registration fee per year or $50 for five years, and many thousands have. At age 75, you can get a lifetime membership for $15. Members receive assistance finding teams in their areas and may subscribe to the *Senior Softball News*, which keeps them up-to-date on tournaments and other news. They are eligible to take part in an annual international tour that takes teams to play ball in foreign lands.

For information: Senior Softball–USA, 2701 K St., Ste. 101A, Sacramento, CA 95816; 916-326-5303; www.senior softball.com.

SOFTBALL WINTER CAMP

Softball Winter Camp "for baby boomers and seniors" is an annual event held every winter in Altamonte Springs, Florida (ten miles from Orlando). Older amateur players gather for five days to train, get batting and fielding practice, play eight umpired games, compete in a minitournament, join an exercise program, and socialize. Men over 50 and beyond at all levels of ability can participate, with wives invited to come along to enjoy the fun. Lunch every day, a couple of breakfasts, an awards banquet, an equipment bag, a team shirt, and a cap are included in the fee as are special hotel rates.

For information: Softball Winter Camp, Active Life Styles, 11465 Kanapali Lane, Boynton Beach, FL 33437; 888-335-3828; www.softballcamp.com.

SENIOR GAMES

HUNTSMAN WORLD SENIOR GAMES

Every October, about 7,000 athletes—men and women, age 50 all the way up to 75 and over, from the U.S. and about 40 other countries—gather in St. George, Utah, for two weeks of competition in 20 individual or team events from basketball, mountain biking, golf, softball, swimming, and tennis to track and field and triathlon, with skill levels from novice to expert. The registration fee (currently $69) includes participation in any of the athletic events and additional perks such as free health screenings, seminars on healthy living, receptions, band concerts, and ceremonial dinners.

For information: Huntsman World Senior Games, 1070 W. 1600 S, St. George, UT 84770; 800-562-1268 or 435-674-0550; www.seniorgames.net.

NATIONAL SENIOR GAMES ASSOCIATION (NSGA)

The NSGA is the organization that sanctions and coordinates the official senior games across the country. It sponsors the Summer National Senior Games/The Senior Olympics in odd-number years, attracting about 12,000 athletes over the age of 50 who compete in 18 sports. The Winter National Senior Games/The Senior Olympics, also held every other year, in even-number years, features competitions in alpine and cross-country skiing, curling, figure skating, ice hockey, and snowshoeing.

To compete in the national games, you must first qualify in authorized state competitions, which means you must be a medal winner in your age group or meet minimum performance standards in time and distance events.

For a free Qualifying State Games Directory, write to NSGA at the address given here or download it from the website. You'll find a representative sample of the games in the following pages.

For information: National Senior Games Association, PO Box 82059, Baton Rouge, LA 70884; 225-766-6316; www.nsga.org.

NATIONAL VETERANS GOLDEN AGE GAMES

These yearly multievent games are open to veterans 55 or older, male or female, who receive care at any VA medical facility in the country. Competitive events in the Open Division include swimming, biking, golf, pentathlon, table tennis, horseshoes, and more and are organized into age categories. Veterans with visual impairments or those who use wheelchairs may compete in their own divisions. In some categories, the winners are eligible to complete in The Senior Olympics. The games are held in a different city every year.

For information: Details and applications are available at your local VA Medical Center. Or 202-745-8615; www.veteransgoldenagegames.org.

STATE AND LOCAL SENIOR GAMES

Most states hold their own senior games once or twice a year and send their best competitors to national events. If you don't find your state among those listed here, that doesn't mean there's no program in your area—many are sponsored by counties, cities, and even local agencies and colleges. Check with your local city, county, or state recreation departments to see what's going on near you, or contact the NSGA for a free list. You can find it, too, on NSGA's website. You don't have to be a serious competitor to enter these games but merely prepared to enjoy yourself. So what if you don't go home with a medal? At the very least, you'll meet other energetic people and have a lot of laughs.

ARIZONA

If you are 50 or more, resident of the state or a visitor, man or woman, beginner or advanced athlete, you are invited to participate in the Arizona Senior Olympics held every year over about two weeks in February. Events include 32 sports from track to golf, biking, and swimming and are held in several venues in the Phoenix metropolitan area. Every two years you may compete in qualifying games for the national Senior Olympics. Festivities and medals are included.

Local senior games are also scheduled throughout the year in many Arizona cities, including Sierra Vista, Flagstaff, Prescott, and Tucson.

For information: Arizona Senior Olympics, PO Box 33278, Phoenix, AZ 85067; 602-261-8765; www.seniorgames.org.

COLORADO

The Senior Winter Games at the Summit take place at Keystone Ski Resort each year during three days in February. Anyone from anywhere who's over 50 and wants to compete against peers is welcome. Events include cross-country skiing, downhill slalom, speed skating, snowshoe races, biathlon, figure skating, and more, plus social activities. Age categories for the competitions begin at 50 to 54 and increase in five-year increments to 90-plus.

The summer Rocky Mountain Senior Games are held in Greeley the first week in June and include more than 20 competitions in sports ranging from basketball and racquetball to golf, rowing, track and field, softball, bowling, cycling, and tennis. A small registration fee includes admission to eight different events, continental breakfast, and snacks. To participate, you must be at least 50, and you can compete no matter where you're from.

For information: Senior Winter Games at the Summit, PO Box 1845, Frisco, CO 80443; 970-453-2461; or Rocky Mountain Senior Games, 1010 6th St., Greeley, CO 80631; 970-350-9433; www.rmseniorgames.com.

CONNECTICUT

The Connecticut Senior Summer Olympics include not only competitive sports events but also a mini–health fair and many physical fitness activities. Residents of Connecticut and neighboring states who are 50-plus get together on the first weekend in June each year for three days of events such as the 5,000-meter run, the 100-yard dash, the mile run, the long jump, swimming, bocci, and tennis. These summer games require a small entrance fee.

The one-day Connecticut Senior Winter Olympics, held in February, are open to anyone from anywhere who's at least 50 and an amateur. The games feature downhill, giant slalom, and cross-country skiing, as well as snowshoe races, and take place at Ski Sundown.

For information: Connecticut Senior Games, Sports Management Group, 290 Roberts St., E. Hartford, CT 06108; 800-528-4588 or 860-528-4588; www.seniorgamesct.org.

FLORIDA

Since 1974, the Golden Age Games have taken place in Sanford every November. Today, they host more than 1,000 athletes for a week of 40 different competitions, plus ceremonies, social events, and entertainment. If you are over 50, you are eligible to participate regardless of residency. In other words, you needn't be a Floridian to compete for the gold, silver, and bronze medals in sports such as basketball, biking, bowling, canoeing, checkers, dance, swimming, tennis, triathlon, track and field, canasta, and croquet. There is an entry fee of $8 for the first event and $2 for each additional event.

For information: Golden Age Games, PO Box 1788, Sanford, FL 32772; 407-302-1010; www.sanford.fl.gov.

MISSOURI

The annual St. Louis Senior Olympics have become an institution in Missouri by now. A five-day event in May that is open to anyone who lives anywhere and is at least 50 years old, it costs a nominal amount and is action-oriented. No knitting contests here—only more than 70 energetic events such as bicycle races, 200-meter races, standing long jumps, golf, basketball, free throw, sprints, tennis (singles and doubles), and swimming.

For information: St. Louis Senior Olympics, JCC, 10 Millstone Campus Dr., St. Louis, MO 63146; 314-432-5705, ext. 3217; www.stlouisseniorolympics.org.

MONTANA

Men and women over the age of 50, from Montana or otherwise, are invited to the Montana Senior Olympics, held every year in June. Events range from archery, bowling, and basketball to swimming, tennis, cycling, and track.

For information: Montana Senior Olympics, 2200 Bridger Dr., Bozeman, MT 59715; 406-586-5543; www.montana seniorolympics.org.

NEW HAMPSHIRE

For a week in August, you can compete with your peers in the annual Granite State Senior Summer Games in Manchester, where you can choose from 15 sporting events ranging from swimming to tennis, track and field, shuffleboard, and table tennis. In alternate even-number years, these are qualifying games for the National Senior Games. Sign up if you are a man or a woman who is at least 50 and in good operating condition. The cost is minimal.

For information: Granite State Senior Games, 11 Stagecoach Way, Manchester, NH 03104; 603-622-9041; www.nhsenior games.org.

NEW JERSEY

Held once a year, the New Jersey Senior Sports Classic games feature more than 1,000 seniors competing in 21 competitive sports such as archery, golf, tennis, and track and field.

For information: SCAN Learning Center, Monmouth Mall, 180 Highway 35 South, Eatontown, NJ 07724; 732-542-1326; www.scannj.com.

NEW YORK

The Empire State Senior Games, open to all New York residents who are 50 or over, are held annually in Cortlandt over four days in June. Winners may qualify for the National Senior Olympics. For a small registration fee, amateur athletes may compete in many events—swimming, bridge, basketball, softball, croquet, track and field, tennis, race-walking, cycling, and more. There are additional fees for golf and bowling. Participants are invited to social events each of the three nights.

For information: Empire State Senior Games, NYS Parks, 6105 E. Seneca Turnpike, Jamesville, NY 13078; 315-492-9654; www.empirestategames.org.

NORTH CAROLINA

After local games are held statewide each year, the winners travel to Raleigh for the North Carolina Senior Games State Finals and, perhaps, on to the national games. Most sports are on the agenda, plus an arts competition that celebrates artists in heritage, literary, performing, and visual arts. The state also sponsors the SilverStriders, a walking club for those 50 or better that gives its members logbooks for tracking progress, gifts and awards, and an annual report of their accomplishments.

For information: North Carolina Senior Games, PO Box 33590, Raleigh, NC 27636; 919-851-5456; www.ncsenior games.org.

PENNSYLVANIA

The Pennsylvania Senior Games "combine sports, recreation, and entertainment with fellowship." You can get some of each if you are a Pennsylvania resident who is 50 or older. The games are held over five days in July at Shippensburg University where you can get lodging and three meals a day at low cost. If you prefer to stay in a motel, you'll get a senior discount.

For information: Keystone State Games, PO Box 1166, Wilkes-Barre, PA 18703; 570-823-3164; www.keystone games.com.

UTAH

The Utah Winter Games, open to everyone whatever their age, abilities, or home addresses, schedules more than 100 free clinics and events all over the state from November to January in a variety of winter sports. It includes a free Senior Ski clinic at Brighton Ski Resort in late November, where skiers over 50 are invited for a day of instruction and fun.

The Utah Summer Games Foundation holds annual Olympic-style competitions every June in 41 events from archery to track and field, all of them open to amateur athletes of all ages and skill levels.

For information: Utah Winter Games, 2175 W. 1700 S, Salt Lake City, UT 84104; 801-975-4515; www.utahwinter games.org. Utah Summer Games, 351 W. University Blvd., Cedar City, UT 84720; 435-865-8421; www.utahsummer games.org.

VERMONT

If you are over 50 years old and an amateur in your sport, you are invited to participate in the Green Mountain Senior Games (GMSG). At the summer games, held throughout the summer months at several locations and at the three-day games at Green Mountain College in Poultney every fall, you may compete in sports ranging from golf and tennis to swimming, walking, softball, biking, basketball, and table tennis. The winter games are held in March and include cross-country and snowshoeing events.

For information: Green Mountain Senior Games, 131 Holden Hill Rd., Weston, VT 05161; 802-824-6521.

VIRGINIA

The Virginia Senior Games are an annual four-day event held each spring on a college campus, where older athletes compete to qualify for the U.S. National Senior Olympics— or just for the fun of it. It is a combination of social events and entertainment with sports competitions, open to anybody over the age of 50. Spouses are invited to come along and enjoy the hospitality, which includes parties, dances, tours of local sites, and other festivities. The fees are low; lodging and meals are cheap; and the sporting events are many, ranging from rope jumping, miniature golf, and riflery to swimming, running, and tennis for age groups from 55 upward.

For information: Virginia Senior Games, Virginia Recreation and Park Society, 6038 Cold Harbor Rd., Mechanicsville, VA 23111; 804-730-9447; www.vrps.com.

15

Adventures on Skis

Downhill skiing is one sport you'd think would appeal only to less mature, less wise, less breakable people. On the contrary, an astounding number of ardent over-50 skiers would much rather glide down mountains than sit around waiting for springtime. In fact, many of us ski more than ever now that we're older because we can go midweek when the crowds are thinner and get impressive discounts on lift tickets, especially after the age of 65. A lot of us, too, are taking up the sport for the first time. Ski schools all over the U.S. and Canada are reporting an increase of older students in beginner classes. More and more seniors are hitting the slopes today.

The truth is, you're never too old to learn how to ski or to improve your technique. Once you get the hang of it, you can ski at your own speed, choosing the terrain, the difficulty level, and the challenge. You can slide down cliffs through narrow icy passes or wend your way slowly down gentle slopes, aided by ever-improving equipment. You'll find clearly marked and carefully groomed trails and sophisticated lifts that take all the work out of getting up the mountain.

For years, ski resorts have fallen all over themselves catering to older skiers, offering discounts on lift tickets, cheaper season passes, and other engaging incentives. In fact, it is a rare ski area that does not give a break to skiers over a certain age. Recently, however, because of the increasing crowds of mature participants, some ski areas have boosted the age of eligibility for discounts or free skiing or have reduced the amount of the discounts. Although the usual age to ride the lifts for nothing remains 70, a couple of resorts have raised it to 80 or 82 before you are given the privilege.

CLUBS FOR MATURE SKIERS
COPPER MOUNTAIN OHG

Members of the Copper Mountain Over the Hill Gang, an independent snow-sports adventure club for people 45+ and spouses of any age, ski in guided groups on Tuesdays, Wednesdays, Saturdays, and Sundays from mid-November to mid-April except for breaks during the major holidays. They get liftline privileges, gather for lunch, and then ski again in the afternoon, ending with an après-ski social for members and guests. Throughout the year, members organize potluck dinners, banquets, hikes, bike rides, golf outings, tennis tournaments, and other activities, and a monthly newsletter keeps members apprised of coming activities. Anybody the right age may join or come as a guest.

Membership dues are $270 for a single, $515 for a couple. For those who don't ski, a summer/social membership is offered for $50 a year. It includes the newsletter and all summer and social activities but does not include skiing with the gang.

For information: OHG, PO Box 3488, Copper Mountain, CO 89443; 800-458-8386 or 970-968-2318, ext. 60886; www.copperohg.com.

THE 100 CLUB

The 100 Club is open to couples whose combined ages total 100 years or more and singles over 50. Club members, beginners to experts, meet on the sundeck at Sunlight Mountain Resort in Glenwood Springs, Colorado, every Wednesday at 10 A.M. and Saturday mornings at the Ullrhof at Snowmass during the season to ski together in groups according to ability and stay for lunch. Guests are welcome. After the ski season ends, members get together for dinner, hiking, biking, or horseback riding. Cost for membership is $12 a year and includes a monthly newsletter.

For information: 100 Club, c/o Hal Sundin, 810 N. Traver Trail, Glenwood Springs, CO 81601; 970-945-0966; www .100clubcolorado.org.

OVER THE HILL GANG (OTHG)

OTHG is a club for energetic, fun-loving individuals over 50 and couples (one spouse must be at least 50) that schedules a wide assortment of guided ski trips every year in this country and abroad. Members—about 6,000, 97 percent of them active skiers—are entitled to reduced rates for lift tickets, lessons, rentals, services, equipment, lodging, car rentals, dining, and transportation at nearly 100 of the top ski areas. At most ski areas, the reduced rates are offered whether or not OTHG members are skiing with the club or on their own.

At eight resorts in the Colorado Rockies, local and visiting members meet regularly to ski in small groups with similar ability, each group led by its own guide. At Steamboat, for example, they gather six days a week during the season. At Vail, they ski together on Mondays; at Breckenridge on Tuesdays; at Winter Park on Wednesdays; at Keystone on Thursdays; at Arapahoe Basin on Mondays; at Loveland on Fridays; at Snowmass on Tuesdays; and at Eldora on fourth Wednesdays. Out-of-town members and anyone else over 50 are invited to come along.

Members who reach their 70th birthday (and are willing to admit it) are part of the "Over 70 Gang," and members who have turned 80 are included in the "Over 80 Gang." They receive special shoulder patches and a discount on their next membership renewal.

When ski season ends, you may join OTHG for other activities including biking, rafting, hiking, and golfing (see Chapter 14).

Annual membership fee: $60 single, $100 per couple (three years for $135 or $210).

For information: Over the Hill Gang International, 1515 N. Tejon St., Dept. G, Colorado Springs, CO 80907; 719-389-0022; www.othgi.com.

SENIORS ALPINE SKI CLUB

A club for skiers 55+, the Seniors Alpine Ski Club, based in Calgary and Edmonton in Canada's Alberta Province, organizes many affordable three- to four-day tours every year to world-class ski areas, as well as day trips to resorts within easy reach of the two cities. The longer tours travel by charter bus, the day-trippers go in car pools, and all get reduced lift-ticket and accommodation prices. When they're not skiing, members attend spring and fall dinner dances and may take part in an annual golf tournament. Although most members live in Alberta, there are many participants from British Columbia and even some northern U.S. states, each paying annual dues of $25. Eight newsletters a year keep them informed about club activities.

For information: Seniors Alpine Ski Club, 1111 Memorial Dr. NW, Calgary, AB T2N 3E4; 403-263-6167; www.seniors alpineskiclub.com.

70+ SKI CLUB

The minute you hit the age of 70, you're eligible to join the 70+ Ski Club for an annual fee of $15 ($18 for couples)—until you turn 90, when you pay nothing. Don't laugh. Among the approximately 4,500 active members, 125 are older than the age of 90. Members get a selection of ski trips and special events every year at ski resorts throughout the United States and Canada and sometimes in Europe and South America. Hunter Mountain in New York hosts the club's annual meeting each March. Here the 70+ Ski Races have become such a popular event that contestants are divided into three age groups: men 70 to 80, women 70 to

80, and anyone over 80. Awards are presented at a gala party at the lodge.

Founded in 1977, the club has always promoted the interests of senior skiers, especially those on limited incomes. Today, largely as a result of its efforts, most ski areas give seniors free or discounted lift tickets.

Proof of age is required with your application to join the club, and you may not apply earlier than two weeks before your 70th birthday. Members receive a patch, a membership card, a periodic newsletter, and a directory of areas around the country that offer discounts or free skiing.

For information: 70+ Ski Club, PO Box 277, North Kingstown, RI 02852; 401-667-2892; www.70plusskiclub .com.

SKIMEISTERS

A group of 55-plus skiers based in Denver, the SkiMeisters ski together at Colorado's Winter Park in small groups led by volunteer guides. They ski on scheduled Wednesdays, Thursdays, and Sundays from November to April. Guided cross-country ski days are included as well as group trips to other resorts. If that's not enough, they get together for social gatherings on Thursday afternoons. With 400 members and a waiting list, the club charges a onetime fee of $100, then $85 a year per person. Guests are permitted, but they may ski with the club only twice during the season. To keep themselves busy when the ski season is over, members get together for biking, hiking, rafting, tennis, and golf.

For information: SkiMeisters, PO Box 62625, Littleton, CO 80162.

THE WILD OLD BUNCH

Skiers who frequent Alta in Utah are advised to search out members of the Wild Old Bunch, a "happily disorganized" informal group of longtime senior Alta regulars who hang out together on the mountain and welcome anyone who wants to join them. There are no rules, no regulations, no meetings. The only requirement is that you're over 55. The group grows haphazardly as members pick up stray mature skiers on the slopes. It congregates for lunch at 11 A.M. at a big round table on the deck of the midmountain Alf's Restaurant on the Sugarloaf side.

For information: Look for the Wild Old Bunch on the slopes or at lunch; www.wildoldbunch.org.

GOOD DEALS FOR SKIERS

The older you are, the less it costs to ski. There's hardly a ski area in North America today that doesn't give mature skiers a break. Many cut the price of lift tickets in half for skiers at age 60 or 65, and stop charging altogether at 70, although a few—Alta and Mammoth Mountain, for example—make you wait until you're 80 to ski free and at Dodge Ridge, it's 82. A few areas charge anybody over the age of 65 only $5 a day for lift tickets, and most make offers on season passes that are hard to refuse. Others plan special senior programs specifically for mature skiers.

To give you an idea of what's out there, here is a sampling of the special senior programs, workshops, and clubs in the states where downhill skiing is big business. This list does not include all areas, of course, so be sure to check out others in locations that interest you. Remember to carry proof of age with you at all times. The ski areas change their pricing policies and programs frequently, so while you can use the following information as a guide, you must do your own research, too.

CALIFORNIA

Every Thursday, Tahoe Donner offers skiers age 55 and over morning or afternoon clinics, a lift ticket, and lunch with top senior instructors. Many of the days are spent at other nearby ski areas.

Squaw Valley USA's Just for Women Ski Clinic, exclusively for women over 50, offers a three-day program every year, usually in January, that includes five hours of lessons by women instructors, exercise, workshops, and evening socials. Those 76 and older ski for free and at age 86, Squaw Valley pays you to ski by giving you $5 in Squaw Bucks, good at shops and restaurants.

COLORADO

Almost every ski area in Colorado offers discounted lift tickets to seniors, usually at 65, and some charge zip after 70. Many also have special programs specifically for mature skiers. Among them are these:

The Aspen/Snowmass and the Aspen Highlands/Buttermilk resort areas gives 70-plus skiers a season pass that allows unlimited skiing on any of the four mountains and discounts on some merchandise. There's no free skiing at Aspen until you're 80.

Breckenridge's Prime Time program for skiers over 50 includes three days of skiing and other activities including dinners and seminars. Members of the local Over the Hill

Gang and out-of-towners over the age of 50 get together here every Tuesday for lunch and a day on the slopes.

OTHG members and 50+ visitors ski together on Thursday mornings at Keystone. At Vail, they do the same on Mondays. Arapahoe on Mondays. Snowmass on Tuesdays. Loveland on Fridays. And every day from Sunday through Friday at Steamboat, where the special deal for 50-plus skiers is a free program. Just show up at 9 A.M. on those days to ski with the group.

Copper Mountain is the headquarters for its own independent Over the Hill Gang (OHG), and members ski with volunteer guides on Tuesdays, Wednesdays, Saturdays, and Sundays. They also party together and participate in other activities including golf outings, bike rides, and tennis tournaments.

Crested Butte's Gray Hares is an informal group of friendly 50-plus cross-country skiers that meets Wednesday mornings at the Nordic Center for a group ski and socializing. They take part in Gray Hares clinics and races and the annual Senior Winter Festival in February that features ski tours, races, snowshoe tours, special events, parties, and a parade.

At Eldora, skiers 65 and older can participate in Senior Ski on Tuesdays for special group lessons. OTHG members ski together on fourth Wednesdays.

Every winter, Purgatory Resort in Durango schedules a couple of one-week Snowmasters Clinics for skiers who are at least 50. It includes breakfast, parties, and on-slope clinics.

There are five Senior Special days each winter at Ski-Cooper when skiers age 55 and beyond get a discount on lift tickets.

Steamboat's special deal for 50-plus skiers, both visitors and local members of OTHG, is a free program every Sunday through Friday. Just show up at 9 A.M. on those days to ski with the group. The 100 Club for singles over 50 or couples with combined ages of 100 or more meets Wednesdays at Sunlight Mountain Resort and Saturdays at Snowmass.

The SkiMeisters ski together at Winter Park every Wednesday, Thursday, and Sunday. A membership club, it has about 400 members and a waiting list.

IDAHO

Sun Valley's Prime Time, a week reserved for older skiers, is scheduled three times each winter. It includes seven nights' lodging, five days of lift tickets or a Nordic trail package, races, parties, and special events. Skiers over 60 pay less for the package than those 59 and under.

Schweitzer Mountain's Prime Timers Club for skiers 55 and over is an informal club whose members ski together several days a week and get together for social gatherings on Thursday afternoons. In addition, there's a bargain senior ski week in March, the Snowmaster's Classic, a week of workshops, clinics, social activities, and race training for older skiers who are seeking to improve their technical abilities.

MAINE

At Sunday River, the Prime Time Club, a midweek ski club for skiers 50 and over, meets at the North Peak Lodge every weekday at 10 A.M. from mid-December through mid-April. Members ski together and join the optional activities such as ski trips to other areas, potluck suppers, parties, and off-season get-togethers.

Sunday River also hosts Go50 Week, a theme week held in January for 50-plus skiers, that gives you five nights slopeside lodging, a five-day lift ticket, daily ski clinics, mountain tours, dinner specials, a reception, and a sock hop.

MICHIGAN

During Silver Streak Week in January, those 55 and up ski free on all five weekdays at Shanty Creek in Bellaire. The rest of the time, they pay teen prices and over 70, nothing at all.

Members of Cannonsburg's Silver Streakers Club for skiers over 50 get cheaper daily lift tickets, season passes, and rental equipment, plus a free lesson and reduced fees for another. The club schedules ski outings on the mountain on Monday, Wednesday, and Saturday mornings and organizes both day trips and overnight trips to other resorts.

The Cross-Country Ski Headquarters in Roscommon gives skiers 55 and up a free facility pass and a free trial of skis or snowshoes during Silver Streak Week in January. The rest of the time, they pay the lower teen prices, and at age 70, nothing at all.

At Caberfae Peaks Ski Resort in Cadillac, every Tuesday, Wednesday, and Thursday (except during the major holiday weeks) are Silver Streak Days, when anybody who is over the age of 50 may ski all day for very little. In addition to the lift ticket, you can also get free rental skis and a one-hour lesson.

Skiers 60 or more can sign up for the Silver Streak Program for free at Crystal Mountain in Thompsonville. It gives you half-price lift tickets, cross-country trail passes, equipment rentals, group lessons, and Nastar racing, except on holidays. And you may ski free if you book midweek lodgings on the mountain.

NEW HAMPSHIRE

It's a rare ski area in this state that does not offer older skiers an impressive break on lift tickets. Many also have special programs for senior skiers.

Waterville Valley's Silver Streak program, now in its 20th year, is open to any downhill or cross-country skier who's 50 or over. Alpine skiers have four mornings a week of guided group skiing, periodic clinics, and reserved parking. Cross-country aficionados get guided tours with the ski patrol. Both groups gather for the après-ski parties on Wednesday afternoons and participate in other special events.

The T.G.I.F. (Thank Goodness I'm Fifty) program at Attitash Bear Peak is designed for mature skiers who want company on the slopes as well as some tips and pointers. It meets Thursday mornings for coffee and a couple of hours of group skiing with an instructor.

Loon Mountain's Flying 50s Plus meets on Thursday and Friday mornings for breakfast and skiing with friends and instructors. Groups form based on ability and energy level and are on the snow for two hours. Other benefits include group trips, races, discounts, and social events. Nonskiing spouses or significant others who enjoy the social activities may join as Social Members.

And at Mount Sunapee, Senior Cruisers get together on Wednesday mornings throughout the season to ski the mountain with their friends and an instructor.

NEW MEXICO

Sign up for a Masters Ski Week for skiers over 50 at Taos Ski Valley and you get six consecutive mornings of instruction, all-day lift tickets for the week, and après-ski seminars. At 80, you ski for free.

NEW YORK

Skiers over 50 are invited to join the Senior Ski Program at Ski Windham for eight weeks of Tuesdays from January to early March. The purpose is to strengthen skiing skills, socialize, and meet new people. Join for all eight weeks or by the day, if you prefer. What you get is morning coffee, guest speakers, four hours a day of on-snow lessons, and a midweek, nonholiday season pass to Ski Windham. For information, call 518-734-5070.

Members of the Fabulous 50 Program at Gore Mountain meet every Thursday morning for six weeks starting in early January for 90-minute group lessons with experienced instructors.

At Whiteface and the Verizon Sports Complex in Lake Placid, the Snowboomer Club welcomes 50-plus skiers who meet for six weeks on Tuesdays and Thursdays from January to March. The Tuesday program for downhill skiers meets at Whiteface at 9 A.M. for a coffee hour and a two-hour group ski. Cross-country skiers gather on Thursday afternoons at the Verizon Sports Complex at Mount Van Hoevenberg for two-hour Nordic coaching sessions followed by a coffee hour.

UTAH

Virtually all of Utah's ski areas give senior skiers reduced rates on lift tickets and stop charging at 70, except Alta, where you must wait until you are 80.

By the way, don't forget to check out Alta's Wild Old Bunch that gets together informally to ski almost every morning. Anybody 55 or over is welcome to join the group on the slopes and then eat an early lunch at the mid-mountain Alf's Restaurant.

As for Brighton Ski Resort, the Senior Workshop, a three-Fridays program for "seasoned skiers" over 50, focuses on terrain, snow conditions, weather, conditioning, and motivation.

VERMONT

Vermont's ski areas were the first to cater to older skiers. It is highly unlikely that there are any resorts there that don't give seniors a decent break on lift tickets and season passes. Along with special rates, several areas offer special senior programs as well. Here's a sample.

Stratton Mountain is home to the Trailblazers, a ski club for about 900 skiers over the age of 50 (and their partners), half of whom are full-time winter residents and the other half weekenders, vacationers, and day-trippers. Membership fee is $30 per person for the season. There's a Friday racing program, weekend ski-togethers, snowshoeing, bridge, a computer group, a kick-off party, several big winter parties, and many informal gatherings. In the summer, members who stick around get together for barbecues and golf. Ski retailers and area restaurants offer specials, and everybody gets a monthly newsletter and weekly e-mail reports on conditions.

At Jay Peak, any skier 55 to 65 is invited to join Silver Peaks, a group that skis together every Tuesday.

The Prime Time Club at Sugarbush offers skiers age 50 years and up, levels five to eight, a chance to meet, ski, and learn with a group of their peers. The club meets Tuesday and Thursday mornings for skiing on a variety of terrains.

Mount Snow's Prime-Time Seniors program, also for skiers and snowboarders 50 and over, meets once a week in February and March and offers clinics and a specialized video as well as resort savings.

The Silver Griffins at Bromley Mountain meet every non-holiday Monday through Friday for group skiing, clinics, fun races, picnics, and parties. Members of the group get preferred parking midweek and discounts on food, equipment, and lessons.

Okemo's Mountain Masters is a Wednesday morning program for advanced downhill skiers (level 4 and up) 50 or older. It provides seven weeks of two-hour small-group sessions with an instructor, plus discounted lunch coupons and discounted access to the pool and fitness center per session at the Jackson Gore Inn.

Mad River Glen does it differently. It offers members of AARP $10 off a full-day lift ticket every Sunday during the season. For over 70s, the first five days of skiing are free.

For seniors who like to ski (downhill or cross-country), snowboard, or snowshoe, Smuggler's Notch 55-Plus Club meets Wednesday mornings for a complimentary breakfast, then heads outdoors for whatever activity members choose, finishing the day with an afternoon presentation by a guest speaker. Those 55 to 69 ski at half price on Wednesdays while those over 70 ski free anytime they want. All are entitled to discounts on rentals, lessons, Nordic trail fees, and merchandise. To join the club, you pay only $25 for the season.

16

Perks in Parks and More Nice Deals

All over the country, enterprising states and cities offer special privileges to the mature population. Often they do it to express their appreciation of our many contributions to society. And sometimes they are trying to attract us and our dollars to their neighborhoods, having discovered that we're always ready to enjoy ourselves and know a good deal when we see one.

But, first, keep in mind:

■ Before you set off for a new place, send ahead for free maps, calendars of events, booklets describing sites and scenes of interest, accommodation guides, and perhaps ·even a list of special discounts or other good things that are available to you. For state-by-state tourism information online, go to the Travel Industry of America's website: www.seeamerica.org.

- Many states offer passes for admission to their state parks and recreation facilities for free or at reduced prices to people who are old enough to have learned how to treat those areas respectfully.
- Following the section on national parks, you'll find information about state park passes and special events in many states. There may be other good deals that have escaped our attention, but these are probably the cream of the crop.

NATIONAL PARKS

AMERICA THE BEAUTIFUL SENIOR PASS

Formerly called the Golden Age Passport, the America the Beautiful Senior Pass is one of the best travel bargains around. Good for a lifetime, it costs only $10 for U.S. citizens or permanent residents who are at least 62 and gives free admission to all federal recreation sites that charge entrance fees. An entire carload of family and friends, whatever their ages, can share the privilege when you enter a park with a per-car fee in a private vehicle, so one pass is enough if you're a couple or a group traveling together. Where a per-person fee is charged, your pass admits you, your spouse, and your children.

It also gets you a 50 percent discount on federal use fees charged for facilities and services such as camping, swimming, boat launching, parking, and tours but it does not cover or reduce special permit fees charged by the concessionaires.

The pass is not available by mail or online but must be purchased in person, so pick yours up at the first park you visit or at a regional office of the National Park Service, the U.S. Forest Service, or the Fish and Wildlife Service. Your driver's license will do just fine as proof of age.

If you already have a plastic Golden Age Passport, you may continue to use it. It's valid for your lifetime. If you have a paper Golden Age Passport and wish to replace it

ESCAPEES CLUB

Escapees is a club dedicated to providing a support network for RVers, full-time or part-time, most of whom are on the far side of 50. It operates 19 RV parks and publishes a bulky bimonthly magazine filled with useful information for travelers who carry their homes with them; organizes rallies in the U.S., Canada, and Mexico; and hosts seminars on RV living. Its regional chapters also coordinate rallies and host get-togethers, and its Birds of a Feather (BOF) groups connect members who have common interests.

Benefits include a discount directory listing about 1,000 commercial parks and campgrounds that provide discounts of 15 percent or more to members, emergency road service, mail-forwarding service, vehicle insurance, parking privileges, and voice message service. After a $10 enrollment fee, the annual membership fee is $60 a year per family with a U.S. address.

The club has established its own CARE Center (Continuing Assistance for Retired Escapees), a separate RV campground where retired members can live independently in their own RVs while receiving medical and living assistance.

For information: Escapees, Inc., 100 Rainbow Dr., Livingston, TX 77351; 888-757-2582 or 936-327-8873; www.escapees.com.

with a new America the Beautiful Senior Pass, you may exchange it free of charge with proof of identification.

If you are under 62, what you need is the America the Beautiful Annual Pass (formerly the National Parks Pass). It costs $80 and is good for a year from the first time you use it. It gives you—and up to three more adults (children under 16 are free) in a private vehicle—free admission to any federal recreation site that charges an entrance fee.

Buy your Annual Pass at park entrances, by telephone, or online. If you are an AARP member, save $5 by ordering it on the club's website.

For information: National Park Service, 202-208-4747; www.nps.gov.

GOOD DEALS FROM THE STATES

Virtually every state has a special senior rate for hunting and fishing licenses for people over a certain age (usually 65). Some states require no license at all for seniors, while others give you a reduced fee (usually half). Most require that you be a resident of the state in order to get these privileges. Most states also offer state park discounts to seniors, usually only residents, reducing or eliminating entrance fees and marking down camping rates. A few have other privileges to offer, such as shopping discounts. To check out the regulations and offers in your state or a state you are visiting, contact the state or local parks department or the state tourism office.

CALIFORNIA

At California State Parks, anybody 62 and over saves $2 on overnight camping fees and $1 on parking. Just show proof of age at the gate. In addition, for $10 seniors may buy an annual Limited Use Golden Bear Pass that gives them free parking at all state-operated parks between Labor Day and Memorial Day.

For information: California Department of Parks and Recreation, 1416 Ninth St., Sacramento, CA 95814; 800-777-0369 or 916-653-6995; www.parks.ca.gov.

COLORADO

The Aspen Leaf Annual Pass entitles Colorado residents 64 and over to free year-round entrance to state parks any day and reduced fees for camping Sundays through Thursdays except on holidays. The pass costs $27 per year.

For information: Colorado Division of State Parks, 1313 Sherman St., Room 618, Denver, CO 80203; 303-866-3437; www.parks.state.co.us.

If you're at least 60 years old and live in Boulder, you're in luck. You may join the Encore program and take advantage of special savings at local businesses, including some restaurants, and participate in many activities from classes to day trips and overnight adventures, special events, and wellness programs. You can join other members in monthly social get-togethers, tennis games, hikes, volleyball, strength training, yoga, water exercise, golf, and workouts, and get special rates on massages and reflexology. Membership costs $20 a year for city residents, $25 for nonresidents, $10 for a second person of the same household.

For information: Encore Boulder Senior Services, 909 Arapahoe Ave., Boulder, CO 80302; 303-441-3148; www.ci.boulder.co.us.

CONNECTICUT

Residents of Connecticut who are over 65 get a free lifetime Charter Oak Pass that gets them free admission into all state parks and forests plus Gillette Castle, Dinosaur Park, and Quinebaug Valley Hatchery. You can get your pass in person at parks all over the state or by mail. Write to the address given and send along a copy of your current Connecticut driver's license.

Inland fishing licenses, too, are free to residents over 65 and are available at any town hall in the state or at the DEP. *For information:* DEP, Charter Oak Pass, State Parks Division, 79 Elm St., Hartford, CT 06106; 860-424-3200; www .dep.state.ct.us.

FLORIDA

Orlando, one of the most popular destinations in the U.S. today, is visited by more than seven million mature travelers a year. To accommodate them, the Orlando Visitors Bureau offers a list of discounts and special rates for visitors age 55 or 65 at almost 100 establishments in the area, including retail stores, hotels, vacation rentals, attractions, and cultural sites. The list is available only on the website.

Whatever your age, be sure to acquire the free Orlando Magicard that's valid for up to six people, any age, and provides even more discounts. Download it from the website or pick it up at the Official Visitor Center at 8723 International Drive.

For information: Orlando/Orange County Convention and Visitors Bureau, 6700 Forum Dr., Orlando, FL 32821; 800-972-3304 or 407-636-5822; www.orlandoinfo.com.

The thick coupon booklet, *$1,000 Worth of the Palm Beaches for Free*, is not exclusively for visitors over 50, but it offers many ways to save money in the off-season (April to mid-December), such as discounts, two-for-one deals, and complimentary offers on shopping, dining, sporting activities, and attractions.

For information: Palm Beach County Convention and Visitors Bureau, 1555 Palm Beach Lakes Blvd., West Palm Beach, FL 33401; 800-833-5733 or 561-233-3000; www .palmbeachfl.com.

HAWAII

Hawaii caters to the over-50 crowd, and there are discounts for almost everything, including hotels, golf courses, rental cars, and movies. If you live in Oahu and are 65-plus, take advantage of an offer from TheBus, the municipal bus system. This is TheBus Senior Annual Pass that costs $30 and may be used for a year of unlimited travel for regular and *Express!* Service.

An alternative is to buy a TheBus Senior Card for $10. This one is good for four years and allows you to pay only $1 per one-way trip. Or simply get on the bus and pay $1, presenting your Medicare card to the driver when you board. Yet another choice is the Visitor Pass for all ages and costs $15 for four days of unlimited travel.

For information: TheBus Pass Office, 811 Middle St., Honolulu, HI 96819; 808-848-5555; www.thebus.org.

ILLINOIS

Residents of Illinois who are 65 or more may ride on all main line and fixed-route buses and trains in the state without paying a cent. That, of course, includes Chicago and environs. Pick up a free senior recuced-fare card at a site near you.

For information: 800-252-8966 or www.illinois.gov/transit.

INDIANA

The Golden Hoosier Passport admits Indiana residents over the age of 60 and fellow passengers in a private vehicle to all state parks and natural resources without charge. An application for the passport, which costs $18 a year, is available at all state parks.

For information: Indiana State Parks Department, 402 W. Washington St., Indianapolis, IN 46204; 800-622-4931 or 317-232-4124; www.in.gov/dnr/parklake/fees.

KANSAS

If you're over 65 and a Kansas resident, show proof of age at the gate and you'll pay only half of the usual adult entry fee at all state parks. In addition, at the same age state residents are no longer required to have a hunting and fishing license, although they must pay for special permits to hunt certain game.

For information: Kansas Department of Wildlife and Parks, 512 SE 25th Ave., Pratt, KS 67124; 620-672-5911; www.kdwp.state.ks.us.

LOUISIANA

Visitors 62 or older, resident or visitor, are admitted free to Louisiana state parks, state historic sites, and preservation areas.

For information: State Parks, PO Box 44426, Baton Rouge, LA 70804; 888-677-1400; www.lastateparks.com.

MAINE

Residents and out-of-state visitors who are 65 or over are admitted free to all state parks in Maine.

A lifetime pass fishing and hunting license will cost you only $8 if you purchase it anytime during the year you turn 70. You must be a state resident to qualify. At 65, your lifetime pass costs $80, and that's a good deal, too.

For information: Maine Bureau of Parks and Lands, 22 State House Station, Augusta, ME 04333; 207-287-3821; www .maine.gov. Maine Department of Inland Fisheries and Wildlife, State House Station 41, Augusta, ME 04333; 207-287-8000; www.maine.gov.

MARYLAND

What you've got in Maryland if you are 65 or older is a fare of 55 cents, about a third off the regular fare, on local buses, light rail lines, and the Metro Subway, and about half off the regular fare on MARC train service. Just show your Medicare card, driver's license, or a valid senior photo ID card. A Senior Day Pass costs $1.20 and lets you ride all day. For this you need the MTA Photo Senior ID card.

Maryland residents can get a free lifetime Golden Age Passport at age 62 for free entry to all state parks that charge service fees and half off the fees for reservations for campgrounds and camper cabins Sunday through Thursday.

For information: MTA, 410-767-3441; www.mtamaryland .com. Maryland Park Service, 580 Taylor Ave., Annapolis,

MD 21401; 800-830-3974 or 410-260-8186; www.dnr.state
.md.us.

MASSACHUSETTS

Pick up a Massachusetts Senior Pass if you're at least 62
years old and you'll get free parking at state parks for the
entire carload whether or not you're the driver. Get the Pass
at a park or by telephone or mail. Have your vehicle plate
number handy.

For information: Massachusetts ParksPass Program, Department of Conservation and Recreation, 251 Causeway St.,
Boston, MA 02114; 617-626-4969; www.mass.gov/DCR/
parkspass.com.

For just 50 cents, all seniors 60 and older may ride the
Breeze buses and seasonal trolleys run by the Cape Cod
Regional Transit Authority. The Breeze serves all major Cape
Cod destinations, including Hyannis, Provincetown, Woods
Hole, and Orleans. Residents of Cape Cod may also enroll
in the dial-a-ride program, reserving in advance and paying
$1.50 per ride plus 5 cents a mile for place-to-place trans-
portation for any purpose.

For information: 800-352-7155; www.thebreeze.info.

Resident or visitor, ou can save yourself a lot of money in
Boston if you acquire a Senior ID Pass after your 65th birthday. It allows you to ride the MBTA subways for 60 cents,
the city buses for 40 cents and the commuter rail line for
half the usual adult fare. Get your free pass at the MBTA
office at Back Bay or Downtown Crossing stations or at periodically some senior centers. Take proof of age with you.

GOOD SAM CLUB

The **Good Sam Club** is an international organization of people who travel in recreational vehicles, mentioned here because the vast majority of those in rolling homes are over 50. Its goal is to make RVing safer, more enjoyable, and less expensive. Among the benefits are 10 percent discounts on nightly fees at more than 1,700 Good Sam parks and campgrounds, plus more discounts on repairs, parts, and accessories at hundreds of service centers.

The club offers a toll-free hotline, a lost key service, a lost pet service, trip routing, mail forwarding, a telephone message service, insurance, a magazine, and campground directories. Most important, it provides low-cost emergency road service anywhere in the U.S. and Canada, including Alaska. Social activities include Good Sam rallies and travel tours and cruises all over the world. And about 2,100 local chapters in the U.S. and Canada hold campouts and meetings and participate in local volunteer projects. Included is a free subscription to *Highways* magazine. Membership is $19 a year per family.

For information: The Good Sam Club, PO Box 6888, Englewood, CO 80155; 800-234-3450; www.goodsamclub.com.

For information: Office for Transportation Access, 145 Dartmouth St., Boston, MA 02116; 617-222-5438.

You may fish and hunt for free in Massachusetts once you're 70 years old if you are a state resident, and if you're between 65 and 69, you'll pay about $10 less than other people for the privilege.

For information: Massachusetts Division of Fisheries and Wildlife, 1 Rabbit Hill Rd., Westborough, MA 01581; 508-792-7270; www.mass.gov/masswildlife.

MICHIGAN

You can get some good deals in Michigan if you are a resident who's reached the age of 65. These include a motor-vehicle permit for $6 a year that gets you into all state parks and a fishing or hunting license for $6 a year.

For information: Department of Natural Resources, Manson Bldg., PO Box 30031, Lansing, MI 48909; 517-373-9900; www.michigan.gov/dnr.

MONTANA

Once you are 62, you may fish and hunt most game birds without charge if you are a resident of the state. In addition, anyone of any age who arrives at the entrance gate to a state park in a car with Montana license plates is admitted without charge.

For information: Montana Fish, Wildlife, and Parks Department, 1420 E. 6th Ave., Helena, MT 59620; 406-444-2535; www.fwp.state.mt.us.

NEVADA

In Carson City, you will strike silver without doing any digging—if you are over 50 and join the free Seniors Strike Silver Club. You'll get a list of discounts in town, plus a membership card to present as identification to participating lodgings.

For information: Carson City Convention & Visitors Bureau, 1900 S. Carson St., Carson City, NV 89701; 800-

NEVADA-1 (800-638-2321) or 775-687-7410; www.carson
-city.org.

NEW HAMPSHIRE

You must be a resident of New Hampshire and at least 65
years old to enter state parks for the day at no charge. You're
also entitled to a discount of $5 per campsite per night. But
you must wait until you are age 68 to get a free permanent license for hunting and fishing, archery, and clam- and
oyster-digging. You forfeit this privilege if you move out of
the state.

For information: New Hampshire Division of Parks &
Recreation, 172 Pembroke Rd., PO Box 1856, Concord, NH
03302; 603-271-3556; www.nhparks.state.nh.us. New Hampshire Fish & Game Department, 11 Hazen Dr., Concord,
NH 03301; 603-271-3421; www.wildnh.com.

NEW JERSEY

If you are at least 65, you may travel at half the regular fare
anytime any day of the week aboard New Jersey Transit
trains and buses. If you're 62 to 64, you'll get the same deal
but only during off-peak hours—9:30 A.M. to 4 P.M. and
7 P.M. to 6 A.M. Either way, just show proof of age, such as
a Medicare card or driver's license, or flash a Reduced Fare
Card.

State residents who are at least 62 years of age are eligible
for free senior citizen passes from the New Jersey Division
of Parks and Forestry. With the pass, you pay nothing for
admission and parking at all state parks, recreation areas,
and historic sites. In addition, the Division of Fish and

Wildlife reduces the cost of a fishing license by about half for those who are 65 to 69, while those at least 70 may fish for $12.50 a year. Hunting license fees are cut in half for seniors 65 and over.

For information: NJ Transit, 800-772-2222; www.njtransit .com. New Jersey Division of Parks and Forestry, 800-843-6420; www.njparksandforests.org. New Jersey Division of Fish and Wildlife, 609-292-2965; www.njfishandwildlife .org.

NEW YORK

Simply by presenting your current valid New York driver's license or a New York nondriver's identification card, you will be entitled to all of the privileges of the Golden Park Program for residents over the age of 62. The program offers, any weekday except holidays, free vehicle access to state parks and arboretums; reduced entrance fees at state historic sites; and reduced fees for state-operated swimming, golf, tennis, and boat rentals.

For information: State Parks, Empire State Pl., Albany, NY 12238; 518-474-0456; www.nysparks.com.

At age 65, you can ride the commuter railroads and most bus lines in New York State for half fare by showing proof of age. In New York City, buses and subways are 50 percent off too, and it costs only $1.50 to ride express buses between the hours of 10 A.M. and 3 P.M. Call for an application and instructions.

By the way, a Fun Pass, good for a day of unlimited travel in New York City, may be purchased by anyone of any age for $7.50. Buy it in any subway station.

For information: New York City Transit Reduced-Fare Line, 718-243-4999; www.mta.nyc.ny.us.

Buffalo's residents who are at least 55 years old are entitled to a Senior Discount Card that will save them money. The free card is accompanied by a booklet listing a couple of hundred participating businesses that offer discounts and other privileges. Call for an application or download it from the city's website.

For information: Division for Senior Services, Room 8A, City Hall, 65 Niagara Square, Buffalo, NY 14202; 716-851-4141; www.city-buffalo.com.

OHIO

You are in luck if you live in Ohio because the minute you turn 60, you may sign up for a free Golden Buckeye Card that gives you discounts on prescription drugs and savings for such things as meals, entertainment, merchandise, and services at thousands of businesses all over the state. Some merchants offer daily discounts, some on certain days of the week, some during certain seasons of the year. Most Ohio residents receive their cards in the mail soon after their 60th birthdays, but if you don't get yours, you can pick one up at most senior centers and public libraries, or call the toll-free number for the location of a sign-up site near you.

For information: Golden Buckeye Card Program, Ohio Dept. of Aging, 50 W. Broad St., 9th floor, Columbus, OH 43215; 800-266-4346 or 614-466-6191; www.goldenbuck eye.com.

When you want to book a room at any of the seven Ohio State Park Resorts, ask for the Super Senior Discount if you are a member of AARP or Ohio's Golden Buckeye program. You are eligible for a 20 percent savings on rooms Sunday through Thursday nights, or 10 percent off on the weekends. Ask for the discount when you make your reservations, and present your membership card when you check in.

For information: Ohio State Park Resorts, 800-282-7275; www.atapark.com.

PENNSYLVANIA

In Pennsylvania, the Lottery Fund pays for many good things for seniors. Among them is free transportation on buses, trolleys, and subways anywhere in the state for anybody 65 or older, resident or not. When you board, you must show proof of age—a Medicare card, a Railroad Retirement Health Insurance Card, or a special Senior Citizen Transit ID Card that's available from any transit provider in Pennsylvania. You may ride for nothing any day, anytime.

On the Southeastern Pennsylvania Transportation Authority (SEPTA) regional rail lines, you may travel for $1 within the state, with no restrictions on day or hour. If your journey takes you into New Jersey or Delaware, however, you pay half the regular adult fare (up to $4 for an advance-purchase ticket). In addition, you can buy a 10-trip ticket at a discount of 15 percent at regional rail ticket offices.

The Shared Ride Program provides door-to-door transportation, usually by van, in Philadelphia and to any location in the surrounding counties within three miles of the city border for a token payment of $4 one way. This privilege is available only to residents of the city who are at least 65. Advance reservations are required for each trip. To register for the program, call CCT Customer Service weekdays at 215-580-7145.

For information: SEPTA Customer Service, 1234 Market St., Philadelphia, PA 19107; 215-580-7800; www.septa.org.

The Phlash Downtown Loop, a purple bus that takes you all over downtown Philadelphia in the summer, stopping at 19 key destinations such as the Philadelphia Museum of Art, is free to anyone who's 65 or older except on weekdays between 4:30 and 5:30 P.M. That means you can hop off and hop on as much as you like, all for nary a cent. Other people must pay $2 a segment or $4 for the day.

For information: Greater Philadelphia Tourism Marketing Corporation, 800-537-7676; www.gophila.com.

PUERTO RICO

When you book accommodations in the slow season at any of Puerto Rico's network of 24 family-owned country inns called paradores (each one is different), be sure to mention that you are 65 or over and you will get 10 percent off the room rate if rooms are available.

For information: Puerto Rico Tourism Company, PO Box 902-3960, San Juan, PR 00902; 800-866-7827; www.goto puertorico.com.

You may travel free on the public buses in the San Juan metropolitan area if you are at least 75 or half price at ages 60 to 74, but you must apply for a Golden Program Pass, only worth the paperwork if you are a resident or a visitor who plans an extended stay.

For information: Call 787-282-7115 or go to the Officina del Programa Dorado in the Terminal de Capetillo in San Juan.

RHODE ISLAND

Turn 65 in Rhode Island and you pay half of the regular fee to use the state beaches weekdays, currently $3 per car for residents, $6 for nonresidents. On weekends and holidays, it's $3.50 and $7 per car, respectively. Season passes are also half price for people 65-plus, now $15 per car for resident seniors, $30 per car for nonresidents. Golf fees at Goddard Memorial State Park are cut in half for you.

At 65, you may also ride half fare except during peak rush hours (7 A.M. to 9 A.M. and 3 P.M. to 6 P.M.) on weekdays aboard Rhode Island Public Transit Authority (RIPTA) buses and trains. For this, you must present a Medicare Card or a RIPTA Reduced Fare ID Pass that is available at the RIPTA Identification Office or at senior centers throughout the state on certain dates.

For information: Rhode Island Department of Environmental Management, 235 Promenade St., Providence, RI 02908; 401-222-6800; www.riparks.com. RIPTA, 265 Melrose St., Providence, RI 02907; 401-784-9500; www.ripta.com.

SOUTH CAROLINA

Residents of South Carolina who are 65 may buy a Palmetto Passport for $25, good for a year. It provides free unlimited admission to all state parks, even the coastal beaches, for the passport holder and everyone riding in the same vehicle. Without the passport, residents 65+ get a reduction of 35 percent off the admission fees, and the same discount on campsites, picnic shelters, greens fees, and fishing piers. You can obtain the pass at a park or the central office of the park service.

Out-of-state visitors are eligible for the discount only at six state parks or may get free admission with an America the Beautiful Senior Pass, issued by the U.S. National Park Service.

If you live in South Carolina and are 65, you are entitled to a free lifetime hunting and fishing license. An excellent deal, especially as others pay a few hundred dollars for the same privileges.

For information: South Carolina Department of Parks, 1205 Pendleton St., Columbia, SC 29201; 803-734-0156. Licenses: Office on Aging, 1301 Gervais St., Columbia, SC 29201; 800-868-9095 or 803-734-9900; www.aging.sc.gov.

TENNESSEE

Anyone over the age of 62, state resident or not, gets a 10 percent discount on food at park restaurants, cabins, and rooms at the Resort Park Inns. Tennessee residents over 62 pay no greens fees at state golf courses on Mondays. They are charged only 50 percent of the regular camping fees, while out-of-state 62-plus campers are entitled to a 10 percent reduction. Admission to all state parks is free, regardless of your age.

For information: Tennessee Parks and Wildlife, 401 Church St., L & C Annex, Nashville, TN 37243; 800-421-6683 or 615-532-0109; www.tnstatepark.com.

TEXAS

The Texas Parklands Passport is free to all comers who are over the age of 65. If you turned 65 on or before September 1, 1995, resident of Texas or not, the passport gives you free admission to state parks. If your 65th birthday was after that date, it admits you to the parks at half price. Pick up your passport at any park.

For information: Texas Parks and Wildlife, 4200 Smith School Rd., Austin, TX 78744; 800-792-1112 or 512-389-4800; www.tpwd.state.tx.us.

If you are a winter snowbird in Galveston, be sure to stop at the Galveston Island Visitor Information Center and sign up for a free Special Winter Texan ID card. It gives you discounts or specials at more than 100 businesses on the island, including accommodations, attractions, auto services, banking services, retail stores, restaurants, medical services, fishing charters, and golf courses.

For information: Galveston Island Visitor Information Center, 2027 61st St., Galveston, TX 77551; 888-425-4753 or 409-763-4311; www.galvestoncvb.com.

UTAH

The Senior Adventure Pass, available to state residents 62 or over, costs $35 a year and allows you and up to seven guests in the same private vehicle day-use admission to all Utah state parks. It also gives you $2 off camping fees seven days a week (excluding holidays and holiday weekends). Get yours at state park entrance booths or at state offices. Or, you can show a Utah driver's license or other legal ID and get a senior discount on the regular day-use entrance fee at any state park.

For information: Utah Department of Parks, 1594 W. North Temple, Salt Lake City, UT 84114; 877-UT-PARKS or 801-538-7220; www.secure.utah.gov/parkspass.

VERMONT

Vermont residents age 62 or over can purchase a Green Mountain Passport for $2 from their own town clerk's office. It is good for a lifetime and entitles them to free admission to all state parks and state-sponsored events. Many local businesses offer discounts on merchandise and services to passport holders. In addition, residents 65-plus can get a lifetime hunting and fishing permit at a discounted cost.

For information: Vermont Department of Human Resources, 103 S. Main St., Waterbury, VT 05671; 802-241-4534; www.dad.state.vt.us. For hunting and fishing: Department of Fish and Wildlife, 802-241-3700.

VIRGINIA

Virginia offers many park passes just for those 62 and older. They include the Senior Lifetime Naturally Yours Passport Plus, good for parking and admission to state parks and discounts on facilities and equipment, which costs $110 but lasts for life; the Senior Parking Passport, $22, valid for a year of parking and admission for your park of choice; and the Senior Park/Launch Passport that comes in various versions.

In this state that abounds with historic sites, you will find senior discounts almost everywhere you go. You will get them, for example, at Colonial Williamsburg, Busch Gardens, Mount Vernon, the Edgar Allen Poe Museum, and the Virginia Air and Space Center.

For information: Virginia State Parks, 203 Governor St., Richmond, VA 23218; 800-933-PARK (in Richmond, 225-3867); www.dcr.state.va.us/parks/passes. For historic sites: Virginia Division of Tourism, 800-932-5827; www.vir ginia.org.

WASHINGTON

If you live in Greater Seattle and you're at least 60 years old, you are eligible for a Gold Card that gives you quick access to the city's Senior Information and Assistance program, 50 percent off on dog and cat licenses, and a free Special Discounts directory listing businesses in Seattle and King County that offer senior discounts. Pick up the Gold Card at the Mayor's Office for Senior Citizens or Seattle Neighborhood Service Centers. The directories are available at public libraries, senior centers, and parks and recreation locations.

For information: Mayor's Office for Senior Citizens, 206-684-0500; www.seattle.gov/humanservices.

For $50, those 62-plus may buy an Off-Season Senior Citizen Pass that gives them free nightly camping or moorage in state parks from October 1 through March 31 and Sunday through Thursday in April.

For information: Washington State Parks, 7150 Cleanwater Dr. SW, PO Box 42650, Olympia, WA 98504; 800-902-8500; www.parks.wa.gov.

WASHINGTON, D.C.

Senior theatergoers are in luck in Washington, D.C., because many theaters—including the Kennedy Center and the

National Theater—offer them discounted tickets, sometimes even at half price. You may usually purchase your tickets in advance, but in some cases, you must wait until the day of the performance.

For information: Check with the theater that interests you.

When you reach 65, resident or visitor, you pay half the regular fare any time of day to ride the buses and trains in the nation's capital and the metropolitan area in Maryland and Virginia. To ride the bus, you must show the driver a Metro Senior ID Card (get it at a Metro sales office or local library) or your Medicare card or photo identification, and pay 50 cents. An alternative is a Metrobus Weekly Senior Pass that costs $6 and allows a week of unlimited bus travel.

To travel by Metrorail's trains for half fare, show your credentials to an agent at a Metro sales office and purchase a $10 Senior Citizen Farecard or a $5 Senior SmarTrip card. The cards may also be ordered online.

For information: Washington Metropolitan Transit Authority, 600 Fifth St. NW, Washington, DC 20001; 202-637-7000; www.metroopensdoors.com.

WEST VIRGINIA

Everybody who turns 60 in West Virginia gets a Golden Mountaineer Discount Card, which entitles the bearer to 10 percent discounts from more than 600 participating merchants and pharmacies. If you don't receive a card in the mail from the state soon after your 60th birthday, you may apply for one at your local senior center or by calling 877-987-3646. Flash the card and save yourself a few dollars.

West Virginia's state parks are free to everyone, no matter what age. Within the state parks, you are entitled (starting at age 60) to a discount of 10 percent on cabins and lodge rooms, camping fees, picnic-shelter reservations, and golfing greens fees. You'll also pay a lower fee for swimming. Be prepared to show proof of your age. West Virginia residents who are 62-plus get a 50 percent reduction on camping fees during the off-season.

For information: West Virginia Bureau of Senior Services, 1900 Kanawha Blvd. East, Charleston, WV 25305; 304-558-3317; www.state.wv.us/seniorservices. West Virginia Department of Parks, 1900 Kanawha Blvd., Charleston, WV 25305; 304-558-2764. Tourism hotline, 800-CALL-WVA (800-225-5982); www.callwva.com.

WISCONSIN

This state's residents who are over the age of 65 pay only half the annual fee for fishing and small-game hunting licenses and for the annual admission sticker that gets them into state parks. On a daily park pass, they save a dollar. Buy the stickers at the entrance to parking areas. Residents over 75 merely have to show proof of age to hunt or fish free.

For information: For hunting and fishing licenses: Wisconsin Department of Natural Resources, PO Box 7924, Madison, WI 53707; 888-936-7463; www.dnr.state.wi.us. For state parks admission stickers: DNR Parks & Recreation, 101 S. Webster St., Madison, WI 53707; 608-266-2621.

17

Shopping Breaks and Other Practical Matters

In this chapter there are no suggestions for interesting vacation possibilities or unusual places to explore. Instead, here's useful information about benefits and services that could be coming to you simply because you are now old enough to take advantage of them.

All over the U.S. and Canada today, and increasingly the rest of the world, retailers offer discounts and other special privileges to older customers. That's because they have come to realize that this huge group of consumers knows the value of a dollar, is extremely fond of bargains, and usually has the will and the time to hunt them down. In fact, the older population has begun to expect reduced prices and to become loyal customers of the shops that offer them.

SAVINGS IN THE STORES

The age at which you can take advantage of your special shopping privileges vary, but most retailers start you off at 55 or 60. Some of them will give you your discount every day, others one day a week, and a few schedule discount days sporadically.

AT THE GROCERY STORE

Even grocery stores and specialty food shops often give its older customers a break. Kroger's, for example, offers shoppers age 55 and over a 10 percent discount off Kroger-brand items every day and 5 percent on other groceries on Wednesdays. The BI-LO grocery chain takes 5 percent off on Wednesdays but not until you are 60. At many Wild Oats Markets, it's 5 to 15 percent off once a week for 60+ customers. Publix Super Stores, with locations all over the South, choose Wednesdays for their 5 percent discount to shoppers over 60.

AT THE PHARMACY

Many pharmacies have plans that will save you money. For example, at age 60 (62 in New Jersey), you may enroll in Rite Aid's free Living More program and receive 10 percent off cash purchases of prescription drugs and on all Rite Aid products every day and other merchandise on Tuesdays. CVS gives seniors without insurance coverage 10 percent off on prescriptions. Longs Drugs, a group of drugstores in the western U.S., has its Senior Advantage program for customers age 55 or 65 who are not covered by insurance, saving them 10 to 50 percent on cash prescriptions and 10 percent on house-brand products. Eckerd's Senior Rewards Card allows 55-plus customers in Texas and Florida to earn 10 percent credit on all cash-paid prescriptions, the credit to be used toward the purchase of any merchandise in the store.

AT RETAIL STORES

Even some major department stores occasionally feature senior savings days, when everything costs 10 or 15 percent less for customers over 60 or thereabouts. Most Banana Republics give older customers 10 percent off every day. Kohl's Department Stores schedules periodic senior days, usually on a Wednesday and announced in local newspapers, when you get 15 percent taken off the cost of your purchases. Ross Dress for Less, with about 500 stores in 22 states, gives shoppers 55-plus the same 10 percent but does it every Tuesday. Many of Modell's sporting-goods stores take 10 percent off for seniors every day of the week. Members of the Club 50 Plus at Peebles and Bealls Department Stores in 33 states are entitled to a 15 to 20 percent discount on all purchases the first Tuesday of the month.

On Tuesdays, Chelsea Premium Outlets offer "50 Plus Shopper Perks" that take 10 percent off their already-discounted fashions to shoppers of the right age. For those age 55, many DressBarn stores knock 10 percent off one day a week, and at Belk Department Stores it's 15 percent off on the first Tuesday of the month.

The Grandparents' Rewards Club is what KB Toys calls its senior program, but you don't have to have grandchildren to qualify. If you're over 50, you can sign up for a free membership card and save 10 percent on your whole order, except for video games and accessories, on Tuesdays.

AND MORE

Check out the possibilities of a senior discount at other businesses, too, because you never know when you might be lucky. Beauty salons and barbershops, for example, frequently cater to their older customers, but, because most of them are individually owned, you must watch their ads or signs and don't forget to ask.

Plumbers, dry cleaners, and mechanics are among other local businesses that often offer discounts. So are many veterinarian clinics and practitioners. Even some car dealerships take money off for parts and service. Ace Hardware Stores frequently give 10 percent discount on Wednesdays to customers over 55.

Fitness clubs usually knock off a small amount for new members who have reached a certain birthday. Gold's Gym, the largest chain of gyms in the world, gives AARP members a lower initial fee and up to 20 percent off other costs. while many company-owned Bally's Total Fitness Clubs deduct $50 to $100 from the initial cost of membership and 10 percent off the monthly fees for those 62 or over.

Most Jiffy Lube auto service centers offer a senior discount of 10 percent, and Midas Auto Service makes it a nationwide policy to take 10 percent off parts and service. STS Tire & Auto Centers Silver Club for those 55+ saves you 5 percent on purchases. Check out the local car wash, another business that often gives seniors a break.

GOOD DEALS IN RESTAURANTS

Lots of restaurants offer special deals to people in their prime, but in most cases you must seek them out yourself by reading the menu, asking at the restaurant, or watching the ads in the local newspapers.

At some big chains, such as the International House of Pancakes, Kentucky Fried Chicken, Bickford's, Pizza Hut, Lyon's, Arby's, Applebee's, TCBY, and Wendy's, there's a recommended corporate policy of senior discounts or special senior menus. For example, your local Applebee's gives you a free Golden Apple card that's good for 10 percent off your meal if you are 55-plus, and Boston Market's 600 restaurants offer a 10 percent discount to seniors. Ponderosa Steakhouse and Denny's have anytime senior menus with smaller portions and prices for diners over 55. Even your local Chinese restaurant might give you 5 or 10 percent off the bill.

Sometimes a senior discount is available anytime you decide to dine, but often it's good only during certain hours or as "early bird" specials before 5:00 or 6:00 P.M. The eligible age varies from 50 to 65, and occasionally a restaurant requires that you sign up for its free senior club that issues you a membership card.

Stop in at a company-owned Burger King before 10:30 A.M. and you'll get free coffee if you're a senior. Check yours out—if it's a participating location, you're in luck. Many McDonald's and Dunkin' Donuts locations will do the same.

Even theme parks have a policy of admitting seniors— usually at age 55 or 60—for a little bit less than the going rate.

What all this means is that, wherever you go, it never hurts to ask whether there are good deals just for you.

HELP ON TAX RETURNS

Assistance in preparing your tax returns is available free from both the Internal Revenue Service and AARP.

The IRS offers Tax Counseling for the Elderly (TCE) for people over 60 and Voluntary Income Tax Assistance (VITA) for younger people with low to moderate income who need help. Trained volunteers provide information and will prepare returns at thousands of sites throughout the country. Watch your local newspaper for a list of sites in your area or call 800-TAX-1040 during tax season, January 2 to April 15. Or consult your local telephone directory under "U.S. Government, Internal Revenue Service" to find a convenient IRS office where walk-in tax assistance is available.

TIPS FROM THE IRS

You'll find useful tips on preparing your tax return in the free booklet, *Older Americans' Tax Guide* (Publication No. 554), published by the IRS. You can get it from your library or local IRS office, or call 800-829-3676. You can also read it or download it on the IRS website: www.irs.gov/publications.

Another way to get help with your income tax return is to turn to AARP's free Tax-Aide Service that operates from February 1 through April 15 every year at thousands of sites nationwide. Trained volunteers offer free one-on-one counseling, as well as telephone and Internet assistance, to low- and middle-income taxpayers.

FOR MEDICAL EMERGENCIES

Concerned about having medical problems away from home? You can take precautions by joining MedicAlert, an emergency medical service. You and your doctors provide critical information about your health and special medical conditions and needs. The data are stored and may be transmitted, if necessary, to medical personnel wherever you are. When you travel, you wear a metal bracelet or neck chain engraved with your personal ID numbers, key medical facts, and the telephone number of a 24-hour emergency response center. Meanwhile MedicAlert will notify designated family contacts to inform them of your situation. Enroll for $39.95; then pay $25 a year thereafter. Your records may be updated as often as necessary at no extra charge.

For information: MedicAlert, 2323 Colorado Ave., Turlock, CA 95382; 800-344-3226 or 209-668-3333; www.medic alert.org.

To locate the Tax-Aide site closest to your home, call 888-227-7669, call your regional or state AARP office, or visit AARP online at www.aarp.org/taxaide. Have your membership number and zip code handy and also your calendar, as an appointment is required. This program also provides 24-hour tax counseling on the Internet all year.

AUTO AND HOMEOWNERS INSURANCE

Among the nice surprises waiting for you on your 50th or 55th birthday is the possibility of paying less for your automobile and homeowners insurance. So try to take advantage of your age when you shop for a new policy or renew an existing one.

Mature drivers get breaks—usually discounts of 5 or 10 percent but sometimes more—because, as a group, they tend to be cautious drivers, much more careful than the younger crowd, having shed their bad habits such as speeding and reckless driving. And, although older drivers total more accidents per mile, they drive fewer miles, have fewer serious accidents, use their seat belts, usually don't operate their cars to commute to work every day in rush-hour traffic, and tend to stay off the roads at night and in bad weather. Therefore, statistically, they have fewer serious accidents per driver than other risk categories do, at least until they are 75, when medical conditions—especially deteriorating vision—may start to kick in, increasing the risk of problems on the road. That's when you might see your rates go up again.

If you're retired or not employed full-time, you may be eligible for another small discount. And check out the possibility of even another break if you have been a policyholder in good standing for several years.

An additional discount—usually 10 percent—applies on some of your automobile coverage in most states when you successfully complete a state-approved defensive-driving course. Among the programs is AARP's 55 Alive Driver Safety Program (call 888-227-7669 for information), an eight-hour classroom refresher that specifically addresses the needs of older drivers with physical and perceptual changes that affect their driving. Open to both AARP members and nonmembers at a cost of $10 per person and taught by volunteers, the course is given locally all over the

GOLDEN OPPORTUNITIES

Log on to seniordiscounts.com for a free website that lists thousands of local and national age-related deals all over the country, even in your own hometown. Name your city, state, or area code, then the business category—from restaurants to car-rental agencies, pharmacies, beauty salons, auto repair shops, movie theaters, and grocery stores—and you will get a list of businesses that offer discounts, along with addresses, telephone numbers, and maps to their locations.

For information: SeniorDiscounts.com, PO Box 14762, Chicago, IL 60614; www.seniordiscounts.com.

country. Defensive-driving courses are offered by other groups, including local high schools and AAA.

Homeowners over a certain age are also considered better risks for insurance claims than younger people because they spend more time at home where they can keep an eye on things and take care of their property. So some companies offer them reductions on premiums.

Although discounts are wonderful and we all love to get them, they aren't everything. Always shop the bottom line when you buy insurance. You may be able to save hundreds of dollars just by shopping around, but you should know what you are getting for your money. If one company charges higher premiums for comparable coverage and then gives you a discount, you have not profited. Get quotes from at least three insurers, going over your list of drivers, vehicles, and specific coverage needs.

Be sure to ask for the discounts that may be coming to you because agents don't always volunteer this information. In addition to your age-related discount, ask about others. Some insurers offer discounts for insuring more than one car on the same policy, clean driving records, antitheft devices, low mileage, more than one policy with the same company, and longtime coverage. And watch out for policies that bump up your costs again when you turn 70.

Remember that insurance regulations and the possibility of age-related discounts differ from state to state as well as company to company. That means you must do your homework to find out whether savings are in your future.

BOOMER BANKING

Many banks offer special incentives and services to customers who have reached the age of 50 or 55. The benefits may include privileges such as a low or no minimum-balance requirement; free checks, traveler's checks, and safe-deposit boxes; elimination of monthly service charges; and reduced fees for cashier's checks or money orders. Some banks even throw in discount eyewear and pharmacy service, accidental-death insurance, social activities, group excursions, seminars, and newsletters.

Among the major banks with age-related programs are Wachovia (Access Fifty Checking), Commerce Bank (50 Plus Club), and SunTrust (Select 50). Many local institutions do the same.

The best way to get information about the incentives offered by your bank or others in your community is to speak to a bank official. Sometimes these special services are not advertised.

LEGAL ASSISTANCE
FREE LEGAL SERVICES

The AARP Legal Services Network (LSN) gives AARP members and their spouses easy access to a list of qualified attorneys in their own communities for free initial consultations for up to 45 minutes on the telephone or in person. In addition to dispensing advice, the participating attorneys can provide basic services such as preparing simple wills, powers of attorney, and living wills for low flat fees and give a 20 percent reduction on their usual rates for other services.

For a list of participating LSN attorneys in your area, go to www.aarp.org/lsn or call 866-330-0753.

LOCAL SENIOR AGENCIES

Call on your local area senior agency, which is required by law to provide legal assistance to older citizens. Yours may help you untangle some puzzling legal problems or at least tell you what services are available to you. Or contact your local bar association for information about referrals or pro bono programs.

MORE LEGAL HELP

The National Academy of Elder Law Attorneys will also help you find an attorney who specializes in working with older clients and their families. Remember to ask about a living will, a health-care proxy, and a health-care power of attorney, all of which you need. Call 520-881-4005 or go to www.naela.com.

18

Volunteer for Great Experiences

If, perhaps for the first time in your life, you have time, expertise, talent, and energy to spare, consider volunteering your services to organizations that could use your help. Plenty of significant work is waiting for you, and more and more older Americans are volunteering as a way of finding fulfillment and helping others both before and after retirement.

If you are looking for a good match between your abilities and an organization that needs them, take a look at the programs described here, all of them specifically seeking the skills and enthusiasm of experienced adults. In addition, there are many organizations that welcome all ages but especially appreciate more experienced volunteers. So look into these as well.

To search for volunteer opportunities by zip code and skills, visit www.seniorcorps.org, the website of Senior

Corps, the umbrella organization for three federal volunteer programs.

But, first, keep in mind:

■ When you file your federal income tax, you can usually deduct unreimbursed expenses incurred while volunteering your services to a charitable organization. You may be able to deduct program fees and reasonable costs for transportation, parking, tolls, meals, lodging, and uniforms. You may not be able to take off all of your travel expenses, meals, and lodging, however, when you spend a significant amount of personal or vacation time before, during, or after a service program, or if you get benefit from your service, such as academic credit.

Unless a volunteer organization is fully funded by the government or some other source, you will have to pay a fee to participate to cover the costs of the project and your expenses as well. The fee ranges from a few hundred dollars to a few thousand.

ELDERHOSTEL SERVICE PROGRAMS

Elderhostel Service Programs tap the experience and expertise of older adults (55 or over) in a long list of short-term volunteer service projects in the U.S., Canada, and elsewhere in the world. Teams of hostelers are paired with nonprofit organizations for a wide variety of service activities, from historical preservation to teaching English to natural-resources conservation, working with children with special needs, participating in archaeological research, and even helping to build affordable housing. No special skill or experience is required, and training is provided on the job. A vol-

SENIOR CORPS

Senior Corps, a government program managed by the Corporation for National and Community Service, matches people over 55 with community projects and organizations that need experienced volunteer help. It also acts as the umbrella organization for three programs: Foster Grandparent Program, Senior Companion Program, and RSVP, each described in this chapter.

For information: Senior Corps, 1201 New York Ave. NW, Washington, DC 20525; 800-424-8867 or 202-606-5000; www.seniorcorps.gov.

unteer 55 or older may be accompanied by an adult who is younger.

Many institutions and organizations—far too many to list here—collaborate with Elderhostel to put mature Americans, retired or not, to work for four days to two weeks per session. These are hosted by such diverse groups as Habitat for Humanity, Oceanic Society Expeditions, the U.S. Forest Service, Global Volunteers, Appalachian Mountain Club, Caribbean Volunteer Expeditions, Hole in the Woods Ranch, Grand Canyon National Park, and many more.

The fee you pay to participate varies with each program and includes full room and board, equipment, social and cultural events, and airfare for services overseas. Only a portion is tax-deductible because you will also attend lectures and participate in field trips.

For information: Elderhostel, 11 Avenue de Lafayette, Boston, MA 02111; 877-426-8056 or 617-426-7788; www.elderhostel.org.

EXPERIENCE CORPS

The Experience Corps, part of the AmeriCorps network of national service programs, recruits older adults to serve as tutors and mentors to inner-city children in urban public elementary schools. Although it began only in 1995, it now runs programs in cooperation with local community organizations in 19 cities around the country. Volunteers, many of whom are retired professionals and must be at least 55 years old, receive training in early childhood education and literacy. They may work half-time or part-time or on an episodic as-needed basis and do not require special previous experience.

For information: Experience Corps, 2120 L St. NW, Washington, DC 20037; 202-478-6190; www.experiencecorps .org.

FAMILY FRIENDS

A national program sponsored by the National Council on Aging, Family Friends recruits volunteers over the age of 55 to work in many locations around the country with children with disabilities, chronic illnesses, or other problems. The volunteers act as caring grandparents, helping the families in whatever ways they can, mostly dealing with children, perhaps foster children or adoptees, at home but occasionally in hospitals, homeless shelters, or Head Start centers. They are asked to serve at least four hours a week and commit themselves to the program for at least a year. Volunteers are reimbursed for expenses incurred.

The local projects are funded by the federal government, corporations, foundations, and local, county, city, or state governments.

WORKING FOR THE ENVIRONMENT

EASI (Environmental Alliance for Senior Involvement) is a nonprofit coalition of about 300 public and private environmental organizations that taps the talents, expertise, and enthusiasm of older adults and puts them to work on projects that protect and improve the environment in their own communities. Volunteers in every state and many foreign countries may put in as much time as they wish on such projects as water-quality monitoring, forest management, pollution prevention, community gardens, brown-fields revitalization, and hazardous-waste disposal.
For information: EASI, 5615 26th St. N, Arlington, VA 22207; 703-241-4927; www.easi.org.

For information: National Council on Aging, 1901 L St. NW, Washington, DC 20036; 202-479-1200; www.ncoa.org.

FOSTER GRANDPARENTS

Foster Grandparents serve as extended family members to children with special or exceptional needs. They provide emotional support to children who have been abused or neglected, mentor troubled teenagers and young mothers, care for premature infants and children with physical disabilities and severe illnesses, and tutor children who lag behind in reading. Volunteers must be 60 or older and have limited incomes. They serve 20 hours a week in schools, hospitals, correctional institutions, day-care facilities, and Head Start centers in their own neighborhoods.

For this, they receive—in addition to the immense satisfaction—modest tax-free stipends to offset their costs, some meals during service, reimbursement for transportation, an annual physical examination, and accident and liability insurance while on duty.

For information: Contact your local Foster Grandparents program or the Senior Corps, 1201 New York Ave. NW, Washington, DC 20525; 800-424-8867 or 202-606-5000; www.seniorcorps.gov.

JEWISH NATIONAL FUND (JNF) CAARI PROGRAM

Each winter, the Jewish National Fund's CAARI (Canadian American Active Retirees in Israel) program sends a group of retired people age 50 and above to Israel to participate in an interactive educational program for periods of 2 to 10 weeks. The volunteers work in schools, hospitals, community agencies, and forests for several hours a day. They also tour the country and, through lectures and guided tours, learn about the history, culture, and current political situation in Israel.

For information: JNF CAARI Program, Missions Dept., 42 E. 69th St., New York, NY 10021; 212-879-9300; www.jnf .org/caari.

NATIONAL EXECUTIVE SERVICE CORPS

This nonprofit organization performs a unique service. It helps other nonprofit organizations solve their problems by providing retired executives with extensive corporate and professional experience to serve as volunteer consultants. Its services are offered in five basic areas—education, health, the arts, social services, and religion—and the assistance covers everything from organizational structure and financial systems to marketing and funding strategy. Volunteers' expenses are covered.

For information: National Executive Service Corps, 55 W. 39 St., New York, NY 10018; 212-269-1234; www.nesc.org.

NATIONAL PARK SERVICE

You can put in as many hours as you like—every day, once a week, or full-time for a week or even a few months—helping out at the country's national parks and wilderness areas when you enlist in the National Park Service's Volunteers in Parks (VIP) program. VIPs are not exclusively people over the age of 50, but a goodly portion of them are older people with time, expertise, talent, and a love for wildlife and wild places. You will not be paid for your hard work but may get reimbursed for out-of-pocket expenses, and other expenses are usually tax-deductible.

The job possibilities are myriad, depending on the park you choose. Some parks would like you to assist archaeologists or botanists in their research; others need you to help maintain and restore trails, drive a shuttle, make wildlife counts, act as guides, patrol the trails, work the computers, or act as campground hosts.

For information: Contact the VIP coordinator at the national park where you would like to volunteer and request an application. Or write to Volunteer Coordinator, National Park Service, 1849 C St. NW, Ste. 3045, Washington, DC 20240; 202-513-7140; www.nps.gov/volunteer.

NATIONAL TRUST WORKING HOLIDAYS

Britain's National Trust, which oversees historic and environmental treasures in the U.K., invites volunteers from all over the world on its low-cost Working Holidays in England, Wales, and Northern Ireland. Their job is to lend a hand for one or two weeks at a time performing such tasks as restoring historic buildings, maintaining footpaths, digging at archaeological sites, repairing dry stone walls, doing conservation surveys, herding goats, or even helping with office work. Most Working Holidays are open to anyone over 18, but some of them—called Oak Holidays—are reserved exclusively for energetic volunteers age 40 or over.

For most holidays, your accommodations will be converted dormitory-style farmhouses, cottages, or apartments, or you may find lodgings of your own. Work is paced to allow ample time to relax, take in the local sights, or go for a stroll. All meals are included, although you may be asked to take a turn cooking dinner.

For information: National Trust Central Volunteering Team, Heelis Dr., Swindon SN2 2NA, England; www.national trust.org.uk/volunteering.

PEACE CORPS

The Peace Corps is actively recruiting older Americans to serve in countries all over the world and hopes to raise its number of volunteers over the age of 50 to at least 15 percent of the total. There is no upper age limit for acceptance.

To become a volunteer, you must be a U.S. citizen and meet basic legal and medical criteria. Some assignments require a college or technical-school degree or an experience equivalent. Married couples are eligible and will be assigned together. Service is typically for two years after three months of training.

What you get in return for your hard work is the chance to travel; an unforgettable living experience in a foreign land; basic expenses; housing; plus technical, language, and cultural training. You will also have the opportunity to use your expertise constructively in fields such as agriculture,

SENIOR ENVIRONMENTAL EMPLOYMENT PROGRAM (SEE)

The SEE Program, administered by the U.S. Environmental Protection Agency, gives qualified people age 55 and over the opportunity to help fight pollution by working part-time or full-time at the EPA in Washington, D.C., in laboratories nationwide, or in regional offices, on a variety of environmental programs that help to protect or clean up the environment. The paid jobs range from clerical to highly specialized technical or professional positions.

For information: SEE Program, U.S. EPA, 1200 Pennsylvania Ave. NW, MC:3650A, Washington, DC 20460; 202-564-0420; www.epa.gov.

business, environment, health, education, and community development.

For information: Peace Corps, 1111 20th St. NW, Washington, DC 20526; 800-424-8580; www.peacecorps.gov.

RETIRED AND SENIOR VOLUNTEER PROGRAM (RSVP)

RSVP matches the interests and skills of men and women over the age of 55 with a diverse range of volunteer activities in their own communities. Volunteers—who may serve anywhere from a few to more than 40 hours a week—may choose to tutor children, renovate homes, build houses, teach English to immigrants, plan community gardens, deliver meals, make hospital visits, work in day-care centers, assist victims of natural disasters, or do whatever their own communities need. They are not paid but may receive reimbursement for meals and transportation.

For information: Contact your local or regional RSVP office or Senior Corps, 1201 New York Ave. NW, Washington, DC 20525; 800-424-8867 or 202-606-5000; www.seniorcorps .gov.

RETIRED TECHNOLOGY VOLUNTEERS (RTV)

RTV, a program created by SeniorNet (see Chapter 13), matches technology-savvy volunteers over the age of 50 with community and nonprofit organizations where they use their skills with computers and the Internet to expand the technological capabilities of the organizations. For example, the volunteers might create and maintain a website, use desktop publishing experience to create a newsletter, train staff to manage e-mail, show them how to network computers, create a database, and run inventory reports. Guides and forums on the RTV website allow others to offer advice and assistance.

For information: SeniorNet, 900 Lafayette St., Santa Clara, CA 95050; 800-747-6848 or 408-615-0699; www.seniornet .org.

SENIOR COMPANIONS

Senior Companions provide assistance and friendship to older adults who are frail, have disabilities, or have serious or terminal illnesses and have difficulty with daily living tasks, helping them to live independently in their own homes or communities. Volunteers must be 60 or older; meet certain income eligibility guidelines; and serve 20 hours a week, usually 4 hours a day Monday through Friday. Although they are not paid, they receive a modest tax-free stipend, reimbursement for transportation, some meals during service, on-duty accident and liability insurance, monthly training, and an annual physical examination.

For information: Senior Corps, 1201 New York Ave. NW, Washington, DC 20525; 800-424-8867 or 202-606-5000; www.seniorcorps.gov.

SERVICE CORPS OF RETIRED EXECUTIVES (SCORE)

A national organization, SCORE offers free counseling for fledgling small businesses by working and retired executives with expertise in a range of areas, including finance, management, and marketing. Its volunteers serve as mentors in one-on-one counseling, computer counseling, seminars, and workshops. SCORE currently has a membership of about 10,500 men and women and 389 chapters all over the country.

For information: Contact your local U.S. Small Business Administration office or SCORE, 409 Third St. SW, 6th floor, Washington, DC 20024; 800-634-0245 or 202-205-6762; www.score.org.

SERVICE OPPORTUNITIES FOR OLDER PEOPLE (SOOP)

SOOP, sponsored by the Mennonite Mission Network and other organizations, provides a way for older people of all religious persuasions to contribute their experience and skills in 23 locations throughout the U.S. and Canada. You may sign up for five weeks or up to six months, living at the site and working to help others in need in whatever way you can, from teaching, building, and child care to home-making, farming, and administering. Once you decide on the kind of work and time commitment you prefer, you make plans with a location coordinator for your assignment and housing. Volunteers usually pay for their own travel, food, and lodging.

For information: Mennonite Mission Network, PO Box 370, Elkhart, IN 46515; 866-866-2872 or 574-294-7523; www .mennonitemission.net.

SHEPHERD'S CENTERS OF AMERICA (SCA)

An interfaith, nonprofit organization of older adults who volunteer their skills to help seniors in their communities, SCA has about 100 centers in the U.S. Supported by Catholic, Jewish, and Protestant congregations as well as businesses and foundations, the centers operate many programs designed to enable older people to remain in their own homes as active participants in community life. They also encourage intergenerational interaction. Centers offer such in-home services as Telephone Visitors, Family Friends, Meals on Wheels, Handyhands Service, and Respite Care, all provided mostly by volunteers. Programs at the centers include other services, day trips, classes, and courses as well as support groups and referrals. Membership is open to anyone over the age of 55.

For information: Shepherd's Centers of America, 1 W. Armour Blvd., Ste. 201, Kansas City, MO 64111; 800-547-7073 or 816-960-2022; www.shepherdcenters.org.

JOB PROGRAM FOR 55+

Senior Community Service Employment Program (SCSEP) is a federally funded program that provides job training for people with limited financial resources who are 55 or older. It pays their salaries while they work part-time getting on-the-job training at nonprofit agencies such as libraries, community centers, and social services. The ultimate goal is placement in permanent jobs in the public or private sector. *For information:* SCSEP, NCOA; 800-424-9046 or 202-479-1200; www.ncoa.org.

SIERRA CLUB

The Sierra Club, the environmental organization, plans some of its volunteer service programs exclusively for people over the age of 50. The programs team you up with rangers and park service personnel to help out with research projects or the maintenance of wilderness areas. The one-week stints are inexpensive, labor-intensive, and sociable, with time allowed for sightseeing and relaxation. You must get yourself to and from the site you've chosen and pay a small fee for the privilege of contributing. You may choose your location and the type of work you want to do, such as trail building, restoring gardens, planting trees, painting and repairing fences, and inventorying songbirds.

Membership in the Sierra Club costs you less if you are a senior—$25 a year instead of the $39 it costs younger adults. Two seniors in the same household may join for $35 a year that otherwise costs $47.

For information: Sierra Club Outings, 85 Second St., San Francisco, CA 94105; 415-977-5521; www.sierraclub.org /outings.

VOLUNTEER SENIOR RANGER CORPS (VSRC)

The VSRC, already operating in about 10 national parks, is a new program established by the National Parks Foundation, the National Park Service, and the Environmental Alliance for Senior Involvement (EASI), with funding from the UPS Foundation. Senior volunteers, who must be at least 50, work together with young people from youth groups and inner-city schools on environmental projects within the parks. Each of the participating parks, including Glacier National Park, Delaware Water Gap National Recreation Area, and Fire Island National Seashore, determine what jobs need to be done, such as restoring native plants, monitoring water and wildlife, and repairing structures and trails.

For information: EASI, 5615 26th St. N, Arlington, VA 22207; 703-241-4927; www.easi.org.

VOLUNTEERS FOR ISRAEL

In this volunteer work-and-cultural program in Israel for adults 18 and older, you'll put in eight-hour days for two to three weeks, working alongside members of the Israel Defense Forces. You'll sleep in a segregated dormitory and work in small groups at a reserve or supply military base, doing whatever needs doing most at that moment. You may serve in supply, warehousing, or maintenance of equipment or in social services in hospitals. You'll wear an army uniform with a "Civilian Volunteer" patch. Board, room, and other expenses are free, but you must pay for your own partially subsidized airfare.

For information: Volunteers for Israel, 330 West 42nd St., New York, NY 10036; 212-643-4848; www.vfi-usa.org.

19

Over-50 Organizations

When you consider that there are more people in this country over the age of 55 than there are children in elementary and high schools, you can see why we have powerful potential to influence what goes on around here. As the demographic discovery of the times, a group that controls most of the nation's disposable income, we are a prime marketing target. And, just like any other large group of people, we've got plenty of needs.

A number of organizations act as advocates for the 50-plus population, providing us with special privileges as well as opportunities to spend our money on their products or services. Here is a brief rundown on them and what they have to offer you. You may want to join more than one so you can get the best of each.

AARP

AARP offers so many benefits that you'd be mighty foolish not to join as soon as you turn 50 and become eligible for membership in this 39-million-member organization that serves as an advocate for the older population and has become one of the most effective lobbying groups in the country. Its informative newsletter, *AARP Bulletin*, and its lively magazine, *AARP The Magazine*, go to more homes than any other publications in the U.S. The cost of membership is $12.50 for a year, $21 for two years, $29.50 for three years, or $39.95 for five years (and that includes your spouse or companion who may be under 50). Overseas members pay $28 per year. Here are some of AARP's benefits:

- Group health insurance, life insurance, automobile insurance, homeowner insurance, mobile-home insurance, long-term-care insurance
- A broad assortment of money-saving discounts on airfares, cruises, hotels and motels, auto rentals, health clubs, vacation packages, entertainment, legal services, online services, and more (to view them, see www.aarp.org/privileges)
- A mail-order pharmacy service that delivers prescription and nonprescription drugs
- A motoring plan that includes emergency road and towing services, trip planning, and other benefits
- A national advocacy and lobbying program at all levels of government to develop legislative priorities and represent the interests of older people

■ About 4,000 local chapters with their own activities and volunteer projects

■ Fully staffed offices in all 50 states plus Puerto Rico and the U.S. Virgin Islands

■ Special programs in a wide range of areas such as consumer affairs, legal counseling, financial information, housing, health advocacy, voter education, employment planning, independent living, disability initiatives, grandparent information, and public benefits

■ Tax-Aide, a program conducted in cooperation with the IRS that helps lower- and moderate-income members with their income tax returns

■ 55 ALIVE Driver Safety Program, an eight-hour course offered nationwide to improve your driving skills and, in many states, help you qualify for a multiyear discount on auto insurance premiums

■ Legal Services Network, which assists members in finding prescreened attorneys to help with legal problems

■ Free publications on many subjects relevant to your life

For information: AARP, 601 E St. NW, Washington, DC 20049; 888-OUR-AARP (888-687-2277) or 202-434-2277; www.aarp.org.

ALLIANCE FOR RETIRED AMERICANS

This organization, created in 2001 by a coalition of the AFL-CIO, affiliated unions, and community-based organizations, is dedicated solely to social and economic justice for seniors and now has about 3 million members. Its purpose is to mobilize millions of older people to influence legislative and political issues important to older citizens. It also gives you benefits including discounts and credit counselors. Annual dues of most union retirees are paid by their unions; others pay a membership fee of $10 a year.

For information: Alliance for Retired Americans, 888 16th St. NW, Washington, DC 20006; 888-373-6497 or 202-637-5399; www.retiredamericans.org.

CANADA'S ASSOCIATION FOR THE FIFTY-PLUS (CARP)

Canadians over the age of 50 are invited to join CARP, a lobbying group with more than 350,000 members, retired and employed. For a membership fee of $19.95 (Canadian) a year for singles or couples, members get many benefits, including discounted rates on out-of-country health insurance, long-term-care insurance, extended health and dental plans, and automobile and home insurance. They can also take advantage of an expanded travel program with an auto club and discounts on travel packages, hotels, and car rentals. Members may also participate in the activities of local chapters in their own communities.

CARP publishes a lively, informative magazine called *Zoomer*, with six regular issues per year, that offers articles on a wide range of subjects such as health care, travel, hobbies, politics, and people. CARP is a major advocate, national and provincial, on issues of great concern to mature Canadians.

For information: CARP, 27 Queen St. East, Ste. 1304, Toronto, ON M5C 2M6; 800-363-9736 (in Canada) or 416-363-8748; www.carp.ca.

CANADIAN SNOWBIRD ASSOCIATION (CSA)

CSA is an organization with about 80,000 members, mainly seniors and retirees, who travel outside Canada for up to six months of the year. As their advocate and lobbying group, CSA addresses issues of concern to traveling Canadian seniors such as health care, absentee voting rights, cross-border problems, residency requirements, U.S. tax laws for Canadians wintering abroad, transporting pets or vehicles, and estate tax rules on Canadian-owned vacation property in the U.S. And it endorses travel insurance as well as out-of-country health insurance.

Membership costs $25 (Canadian) per household a year, and benefits include a magazine, travel offerings, an automobile club, a currency-exchange program, home and automobile insurance, and social gatherings in popular snowbird locations such as Florida, Arizona, Texas, and California.

For information: Canadian Snowbird Association, 180 Lesmill Rd., Toronto, ON M3B 2T5; 800-265-3200 or 416-391-9000; www.snowbirds.org.

CATHOLIC GOLDEN AGE (CGA)

A Catholic nonprofit organization that is concerned with issues affecting older citizens, such as health care, housing, and Social Security benefits, CGA has well over a million members and more than 200 chapters throughout the country. It offers many good things to its members, who must be over 50. These include spiritual benefits, such as masses and prayers worldwide, and practical benefits, such as discounts on hotels, campgrounds, and car rentals.

Other offerings include group insurance plans, pilgrimage and group travel programs, and an automobile club. A new benefit program is Access to Care that offers discounts on the cost of long-term-care facilities, assisted-living facilities, and home health care. Another is the Health Care Card that allows members to save money on the costs of prescriptions as well as on vision, dental, and hearing services. Membership costs $12 a year or $28 for three years.

For information: Catholic Golden Age, PO Box 249, Olyphant, PA 18447; 800-836-5699; www.catholicgoldenage .org.

GRAY PANTHERS

A national organization of about 20,000 intergenerational activists, the Gray Panthers work on multiple issues that include peace, jobs for all, antidiscrimination (ageism, sexism, racism), family security, the environment, campaign reform, preservation of Social Security, health care, and housing. They are active in more than 50 local networks across the U.S. in their efforts to promote social justice. Annual membership is $20.

For information: Gray Panthers, 1612 K St. NW, Washington, DC 20006; 800-280-5362 or 202-737-6637; www.gray panthers.org.

MILITARY OFFICERS ASSOCIATION OF AMERICA (MOAA)

This independent nonprofit organization is open to anyone who is an active or retired commissioned or warrant officer in any of the seven U.S. uniformed services, including the National Guard and Reserve. Members receive lobbying representation on Capitol Hill and a bimonthly magazine, plus a number of other benefits including discounts on car rentals and motel lodgings, a travel program with military fares, group health and life insurance plans, and a loan program.

MOAA has more than 420 local chapters, each with its own activities and membership fees. Annual dues to the national organization are $24. Auxiliary membership is offered to members' spouses, widows, or widowers, who pay $15 a year.

For information: MOAA, 201 N. Washington St., Alexandria, VA 22314; 800-234-6622 or 703-549-2311; www .moaa.org.

NATIONAL ASSOCIATION OF RETIRED FEDERAL EMPLOYEES (NARFE)

As you can probably gather, this is an association of federal government retirees, current employees, and their spouses, about 400,000 in all. The primary purpose of NARFE is to protect the earned benefits of retired federal employees, and it has become an active lobby program in Washington and throughout the states. Annual membership costs $33, plus local chapter dues. Members receive a monthly magazine and are entitled to discounts and special services.

For information: NARFE, 606 N. Washington St., Alexandria, VA 22314; 800-627-3394 or 703-838-7760; www .narfe.org.

NATIONAL COMMITTEE TO PRESERVE SOCIAL SECURITY AND MEDICARE (NCPSSM)

NCPSSM is a grassroots education and advocacy group "devoted to the retirement future" of Americans with the goal of protecting and enhancing the two major federal programs for seniors, Social Security and Medicare. Its current major concerns are "the preservation of the Social Security system without privatization and the addition of an affordable, voluntary, and universal prescription drug benefit to Medicare as well as the expansion of Medicare to cover new preventive services."

Members, who pay $12 a year, receive consumer information, trimonthly newsletters, a Congressional scorecard guide, invitations to events and programs, and a chance to voice their concerns and opinions.

For information: NCPSSM, 10 G St. NE, Ste. 600, Washington, DC 20004; 800-966-1935; www.ncpssm.org.

NATIONAL EDUCATION ASSOCIATION (NEA-RETIRED)

With a membership of almost three million retired education employees from teachers to school bus drivers, NEA-Retired acts as an advocate for their special interests such as pensions and health care and supports public education through legislative lobbying as well as reading programs, mentoring, and intergenerational activities. Among its membership benefits are life, health, disability, and casualty insurance programs; savings and investment plans; credit and loan programs; discounts; educational guides; and a bimonthly magazine, *Active Life*. Join for $25 a year or $200 for life, plus local dues that vary depending on your state. *For information:* NEA-Retired, 1201 16th St. NW, Washington, DC 20036; 202-833-4000; www.nea.org/retired.

OLDER WOMEN'S LEAGUE (OWL)

OWL is a national nonprofit nonpartisan organization with a network of local chapters that focus on "issues unique to women as they age," such as Social Security, health care, retirement benefits, employment discrimination, and affordable housing. Through research, education, and advocacy activities, it seeks to be a strong voice for the millions of midlife and older American women. *For information:* OWL, 3300 N. Fairfax Dr., Arlington, VA 22201; 703-812-7990; www.owl-national.org.

Index